Looking Closely and Listening Carefully

Looking Closely and Listening Carefully

Learning Literacy through Inquiry

Heidi Mills
University of South Carolina

Timothy O'Keefe
Center for Inquiry, Columbia, South Carolina

Louise B. Jennings
University of South Carolina

National Council of Teachers of English
1111 W. Kenyon Road, Urbana, Illinois 61801-1096

Staff Editors: Bonny Graham

Interior Design: Doug Burnett

Cover Design: Pat Mayer

NCTE Stock Number: 30305

Library of Congress Cataloging-in-Publication Data

Mills, Heidi.

    Looking closely and listening carefully : learning literacy through inquiry / Heidi Mills, Timothy O'Keefe, Louise B. Jennings.

        p. cm.

"NCTE stock number: 30305-3050"—T.p. verso.

Includes bibliographical references and index.

    ISBN 0-8141-3030-5

    1. Language arts (Elementary) 2. Inquiry (Theory of knowledge) I. O'Keefe, Timothy. II. Jennings, Louise B. III. National Council of Teachers of English. IV. Title.

    LB1576.M525 2004

    372.6—dc22

                                   2003026885

To our brilliant colleagues at the Center for Inquiry. We are who we are today because we have been blessed by the opportunity to live and learn alongside you.

Contents

Foreword

Painters, dancers, and musicians frequent museums and theaters to experience and envision what's possible in their working lives. It is rare that teachers are afforded this luxury. We are closeted in rooms with our students and settle for swapping stories with colleagues and friends. Once in a while, however, a book comes along that is written with such passion and detail that we are able to free ourselves from what is familiar and feel, hear, see, and experience new possibilities for crafting our teaching lives. *Looking Closely and Listening Carefully* is one such book. In this text, Heidi Mills, Tim O'Keefe, and Louise Jennings graciously invite us, as teacher-readers, to cross the threshold into Tim's classroom and join him and his students in their remarkable learning community. Here we observe firsthand a teacher who has developed his craft to a level that inspires yet makes visible the complexities that confront even the most experienced teacher. One minute we observe Tim in the midst of his young writers, mathematicians, and scientists orchestrating conversations that seem almost unimaginable to those of us who have worked with young children. The next minute we see Tim standing alone at the end of a busy day, staring at his messy classroom and wondering why he didn't ask the students to pitch in and put things away. And so the story goes, the brilliance of one teacher and his students interspersed with the realities of everyday life.

In reading *Looking Closely and Listening Carefully*, Heidi establishes the theoretical foundation in the introduction and then carefully walks us through the typical daily structures and strategies in Tim's classroom. Tim takes us on a journey across the lives of two students over the course of two school years as he loops with his students. Additionally, Tim writes the closing chapter as a letter to teachers, describing his successes, struggles, and commitment to collaboration with parents and colleagues. Louise takes a close look at the democratic practices that pervade Tim's classroom community. These experiences illuminate John Dewey's claim that education is not preparation for life, but life itself. On almost every page, we observe Tim and his students living life to its fullest by engaging in problems and inquiries that are real and significant to them. These experiences run the gamut from planning the day's agenda to observing and recording wonderings about the natural world. In each instance, students are called upon to make meaning and share interpretations of these experiences. Throughout this process, they, along with Tim, help one another clarify meanings, explore new possibilities, and uncover and question new understandings about their worlds. Tim's responsive teaching supports, clarifies, and nudges students' creative acts of expression as they experience life and make reality for themselves. Tim and his students are present to one another as partners, collaborating to enrich life and learning. Their trust and respect liberate them to make unique and lasting contributions to the learning community. Throughout the book, we hear students speaking freely and openly, entertaining the ideas of others without fear of rejection. Their language is conversational and tolerant of ambiguity. Through remarkable teaching and learning, students' lives are claimed and nourished.

Tim's commitment to progressive practices and his refusal to settle for what's typical is also impressive, especially in today's oppressive climate in which teaching practices are defined by standardized curricula and measured by how well children score on state and local tests. Tim's classroom and those of his colleagues at the Center for Inquiry illustrate what can happen when hard work and imagination come together for the purpose of preserving what people believe in. These teachers choose to work within the public school system; they abide by the same standards as other public schools in their state and district; and yet their commitment to collaboration, a generative curriculum, and student and teacher inquiries never wavers. Their belief that children's lives provide rich intellectual resources for learning and growing never falters.

This book is for educators who continue to hope, who want to open up possibilities for improving the quality of life in their classrooms and schools, and who have the courage to keep their dream alive. The authors do not offer solutions or formulas. They do, however, present, in a strong but cautious narrative voice, a vision of what's possible. Their story makes visible the complex and multileveled understanding of the challenges facing educators who believe, like Dewey, that education is life itself.

Karen Smith and Ralph Peterson

Preface

A Closer Look

It has been more than ten years since the publication of *Looking Closely*. So much has changed since then. Our profession has been under attack much of the intervening time. As a profession, we have been critiqued by those who have political agendas that conflict with the values inherent in progressive education. We have also been critiqued by those who embrace our beliefs but who have found it difficult to imagine practices that are both theoretically sound and practically relevant. And most important, we have engaged in self-critique. We have grown. Sometimes the push came from others. We have learned to listen to questions that teachers, parents, and administrators ask. We have been challenged by critical theorists who pushed us to ask new questions of ourselves and the profession at large. We have also grown from the inside out, through powerful professional development opportunities. Teacher inquiry meetings over the past six years have made it possible to see our students, colleagues, and distant teachers with new eyes.

This book reflects our growth. As such, it builds on lessons learned and shared in *Looking Closely* (Mills, O'Keefe, & Stephens, 1992). Here we take another close look at Tim's literacy instruction and the ways in which his most recent second and third graders have grown and changed as readers, writers, and community members by living and learning together in an inquiry-based classroom.

Our Roles

Before introducing the book in general, it is important to describe our roles as colleagues and authors. Tim O'Keefe is a second and third grade teacher at the Center for Inquiry (CFI) in Richland District Two, Columbia, South Carolina. The Center is a small elementary magnet program that was established as a partnership between Richland District Two and the University of South Carolina (USC). Since the publication of *Looking Closely*, Tim has been involved in a number of writing and video projects focusing on literacy, mathematics, and science instruction in inquiry-based classrooms. Heidi Mills is the curriculum and development specialist at the Center and professor of elementary education at USC. She and Tim have been engaged in collaborative research for seventeen years in various settings. She also works closely with the other teachers at the Center and fosters teacher inquiry through weekly "curricular conversations" (Jennings, 2001; Mills, 2001a). Six years ago Tim, Heidi, and their CFI colleagues welcomed Louise Jennings, an ethnographer and associate professor in education at USC, to the Center for Inquiry. She played an important role at the Center by carefully studying one group of children from kindergarten through fifth grade (Jennings, Karvonen, Kjervfe, Mills, & Ness, 2003; Jennings, 2002; Jennings, O'Keefe, & Shamlin, 1999). Louise started with the first group of CFI kindergarten children in Michele Shamlin's classroom and followed them as second and third graders with Tim O'Keefe and as fourth and fifth graders in Julie Riley Waugh's room. Stories and strategies featured in Louise's chapter took place when she was working alongside Tim as he taught second and third grade.

The Center for Inquiry: A Special School

For the past seven years, Tim has been teaching in the second and third grade loop at the Center for Inquiry. In fact, Tim was one of the founding members of the Center. While it is still a relatively new school, it is so comfortable and inviting that it feels like home. All of the students who attend Richland District Two schools are eligible to apply to the Center through a random lottery. Sixty-five percent of the students are European American, 30 percent are African American, and the remaining 5 percent are from other ethnic groups. We are proud to serve a student population that reflects the diversity of the district in Columbia, South Carolina.

The Center is a special school—the school of our professional dreams. The Center for Inquiry is an amazing place for lots of reasons. Most important, it is a rich place to live and learn because inquiry pervades the lives of teachers, parents, administrators, and university partners (Mills & Donnelly, 2001). While Tim has always felt a sense of professional empowerment and has maintained a commitment to teach in ways he believes in, for the first time he is now in a school where all of his colleagues embrace a shared philosophy. It is a place where the teachers, the principal, and Heidi, the curriculum specialist and university partner, meet weekly for curricular conversations. Heidi plans and orchestrates these conversations by using data she collects as she works across classrooms. During these teacher inquiry meetings, we watch and respond to videos of teachers and kids at work; discuss student artifacts; pose challenging questions for one another, the school, and the profession at large; explore the issues that keep teachers awake at night;

and celebrate the right to think and work together as professionals. As Julie Riley Waugh, CFI's current fourth-grade teacher, described it, "This place feeds me." And it feeds everyone who lives and learns together there. The most experienced teachers learn as much from theorizing about their colleagues' practices as they do from reflecting on their own. In fact, Brent Petersen, a second-year teacher of fourth grade, was validated recently when Dori Gilbert, another founding teacher, raved about all the things she had learned from watching a video of his classroom.

We share the importance of our curricular conversations in this book because the chance to think deeply about our beliefs and practices on a regular basis is a gift that has promoted growth and change for us all. It has helped Tim grow as a teacher and helped Heidi and Louise see more in his teaching. For readers who are interested in establishing teacher inquiry groups, see "When Teachers Have Time to Talk: The Value of Curricular Conversations" in the September 2001 issue of *Language Arts* (Mills, 2001b) and "Inquiry for Professional Development and School Renewal" in *From the Ground Up: Creating a Culture of Inquiry* (Mills & Donnelly, 2001). We also recommend *From the Ground Up* for readers who are interested in the principles and practices of the school in general.

Overview of the Book

While the book clearly features Tim and his students, it is written in third person for clarity and consistency across chapters. We are careful, however, to make Tim's voice and perspective visible through interviews, classroom vignettes, authentic classroom dialogue, and a closing chapter written in first person by Tim. Although Heidi and Louise have been careful to select telling cases that truly represent the essence of teaching and learning in Tim's room, Tim feels compelled to speak directly to you as a reader first. As a classroom teacher, he knows that everything seems cleaner, easier, and neater when it is in written form than it often feels when he is in the midst of it all with his students. The following note from Tim is included so that he might speak directly to teachers who share his joy, pain, tentativeness, and sense of satisfaction in the complex world of teaching.

A Note from Tim

I don't know about you, but it is hard for me to read some of the current literature about classrooms that run like clockwork, where the children behave perfectly and every decision the teacher makes is the exact right one. While reading some of the drafts of our own book, I was frankly uncomfortable. There *are* moments of brilliance in my room. Lots of them. Every year wonderful things happen. My students and I experience fantastic moments of discovery and fascinating conversations. In all of the diverse classrooms in which I have had the honor and privilege of teaching, I have been constantly impressed by the insights and connections made by my students. What makes me a little uncomfortable about parts of this book is the fact that the stories are almost too perfect. The dialogue sounds almost staged.

In a sense, Heidi, Louise, and I are collectors. We collect moments of brilliance and stories in which the potential for learning and teaching are actualized. Of course, we also collect stories in which the outcomes aren't all that exceptional. It is important for me to tell you that there are plenty of times when the life in our classroom is very routine. Sometimes lessons and invitations I have planned simply don't go well so I "bail out" in order not to waste more of anyone's time. I have ended strategy sharing sessions and thought, "That sure was a bomb," or listened to a tape of classroom interaction and wondered after hearing myself, "What was I thinking when I said that?!"

Many classroom conversations are not exactly neat and tidy, with a beginning, middle, and end. Some questions come up but never get answered. Some problems are posed and left hanging. Yes, I have concerns about management, and it remains an area I have to work hard on. Sometimes my students don't do their homework and I'm not sure if their parents read my correspondence. There are typos in some of my newsletters (far fewer now, however, with modern technology).

Sometimes, at the end of the day after hurrying my students outside, the classroom is a mess and I ask myself why I didn't ask everyone to pitch in and help put things away. In short, I am a normal teacher with normal students. I wrestle with many of the same issues other teachers struggle with. My classroom is messy at times, literally and figuratively. I don't apologize. Teaching can be pretty messy. I just wanted you to know that while these stories and vignettes are of the variety that might make my classroom seem perfect, I make the same mistakes as the next teacher.

The stories in this book are true. The dialogue comes from video- and audiotapes and transcripts. The student samples are written by the children's own hands. The stories we chose to share are those that illustrate the potential of teaching and learning in an atmosphere where children are encouraged to teach and learn with and from one another.

Description of Each Chapter

The book contains five chapters. The symbiotic relationship between language and inquiry is featured in the first chapter. We introduce the theoretical framework for the book and demonstrate its explanatory power by revisiting a classroom vignette from the transition first-grade classroom featured in *Looking Closely* (Mills, O'Keefe, & Stephens, 1992).

Chapter 2 highlights the ways in which children learn language, learn about language, and learn through language through daily curricular structures in Tim's second- and third-grade classroom at the Center for Inquiry. In so doing, we examine the ways in which children grow in oral and written language through inquiry and the ways in which an inquiry stance is strengthened through rich, authentic literacy engagements. We walk readers through the curricular structures that Tim uses day in and day out. We delineate the theoretical and practical foundation of each structure and then show what it looks and sounds like using classroom vignettes, transcripts, and student artifacts. We also discuss our current stance regarding the role of the English language arts standards in Tim's room, the Center for Inquiry, and the state of South Carolina.

Chapter 3 features the literacy growth of two very diverse children. We describe the unique paths each child took, while also focusing on the universal learning processes and teaching strategies that made a difference for both children as they were learning language, learning about language, and using language to learn. We show how children grow and change over time in inquiry-based classrooms. Additionally, we share excerpts from our CFI progress reports and student work samples to feature the importance of careful kidwatching and responsive teaching.

Chapter 4 features the strategies that Tim employs to build a democratic classroom community. Since talk is at the heart of an inquiry-based curriculum, it is critical that we think carefully about the nature of talk and the ways in which children support one another through inquiry. Examples of the ways children learn, learn about, and learn through literacy, as well as use literacy to critique, are woven into instructional and community-building strategies. We examine the ways in which Tim and his children build community and knowledge together; create a compassionate and caring atmosphere; use music as a teaching tool and as the glue that holds the classroom structures together; learn to reflect on, critique, and express opinions through language; and share in responsibilities to participate in the classroom.

Chapter 5 is written in first person by Tim, in letter form, directly to other classroom teachers. Tim believes it is essential to close the book with an honest discussion about his struggles and successes as a teacher. His collaborators and coauthors describe the remarkable things that children do in his classroom throughout the book. Tim wants to make sure that readers don't develop an unrealistic vision of his teaching or the student population. He also wants to speak about the importance of collaborating with teachers and parents when developing an inquiry-based curriculum. In this closing chapter, Tim passionately describes the central role of colleagues and parents in his teaching life and reflects on critical insights and strategies that have made a difference when working with colleagues and parents. This chapter contains stories from the classroom and sample newsletters. It reflects important incidents from Tim's past as well as current teaching experiences. Together, the stories and strategies demonstrate the rich and complementary relationship between literacy and inquiry. They also show what happens when teachers have a passion for their students and for learning.

It is our hope that this text contributes to professional conversations about the relationship between inquiry and literacy. We also strive to show the importance of looking closely and listening carefully within classrooms where teachers are working hard to demonstrate what is possible. So often we settle for what is typical in our field. Let this book be one example of what is possible when teachers, parents, university partners, and children inquire together.

Acknowledgments

This book reflects so much more than our combined minds, experiences, and expertise. We have had the privilege of working collaboratively with a number of thoughtful and caring educators, all of whom have touched us in important ways. The Center for Inquiry is a special place. It is the school of our dreams because of the people who created it and who inhabit it today. We are grateful to Amy Donnelly, founding principal, for her work in helping us establish so many of the principles and practices that have become a part of our school culture. We are thankful for Debra Hamm, the original chief academic officer in Richland District Two, for valuing our vision for the Center and bringing it to life. We are also thankful for Charlene Herring, our current chief academic officer, who warmly embraced our school when she inherited it with her new position. Additionally, Charlene worked to help our principal and teachers, as well as a critical mass of others in Richland School District Two, receive National Board certification. We also want to thank Steve Hefner, the superintendent of Richland School District Two, who has astonished us with his wisdom and support. He is a remarkable leader, and we are appreciative of all he has done to make the university-public school partnership work. His support has made all the difference in the world.

The Center for Inquiry is a powerful school because it is a place where teachers matter. We want to thank all of the teachers who have worked at CFI and who have touched us and our students. Several teachers—Michele Shamlin, Rick DuVall, Diana Stout, Monica Faller, and Tammy Ballard—have moved on to make a difference elsewhere but will always be a part of the Center.

We have had the genuine privilege of working closely with the current faculty at CFI for the past four years. And these four years have been the most personally and professionally satisfying of our careers. We owe it all to Dori Gilbert, Jennifer Barnes, Susanne Pender, Brent Petersen, Julie Waugh, and Lyn Z. Mueller. When this collection of hearts and minds came together, everything came together. Our current colleagues are accomplished teachers whose questions and stories inspire us and push us forward. We could never ask for a more professional and caring group of peers.

Lyn Z. Mueller, our current principal, has nurtured each of us in a calm and steady way. It is comforting to know that she is there for us individually and collectively. When Lyn became our principal, we instantly knew it was meant to be. It felt like she had finally come home. Dori Gilbert, kindergarten and first-grade teacher, brings a serious joy to our lives and those she teaches. Dori takes our breath away when we watch her teach. Her work with children and passion for our school set the standard for us all. Jennifer Barnes, kindergarten and first-grade teacher, continually reminds us to delight in children's learning. She brings goodness and insight to our curricular conversations through her classroom stories. Tim has the gift of inheriting children who love to read and write because they have spent two years in Jennifer's classroom. Susanne Pender, second- and third-grade teacher, is one of the most caring teachers we know. She lives a compassionate life in and outside of the classroom. She sees the best and the potential in every child. Susanne also reminds us of what is possible when we create curriculum in concert with the children. Brent Petersen, fourth- and fifth-grade teacher, shows us and his students the value of thinking and playing hard. He adds incredible energy to our curricular conversations. Brent asks the hard questions about curriculum and management and pushes us to explore them together. He is a natural teacher. Julie Waugh, fourth- and fifth-grade teacher, lives her model out loud. She is one of the most empowered teachers we know, one who can present her thinking in bold, provocative ways. Additionally, Julie has developed special expertise in using primary sources to foster inquiry and has mentored us all in this area.

It has been a privilege to work with Jaretta Belcher, our exquisite kindergarten assistant. Jaretta has provided exceptional support through careful kidwatching, working with children, and collaboration with both kindergarten teachers. She makes a genuine difference. Sherry Grosso has also made a difference as a devoted parent, personal CFI chef, and technology instructor. She has nourished our hearts, minds, and bodies.

While the teachers, principal, and university partner work closely, we are all supported by Angie DeBeaugrine and Judi Beacham. Angie, devoted parent and teaching assistant, is one of the most efficient and effective members of the staff. One minute she is assisting with a complex task in the office and the next minute she is coaching a child in writing workshop. She does it all with a smile. Judi Beacham, secretary, orchestrates the office while enthusiastically promoting the school. She loves the Center for Inquiry and tells everyone she knows. We truly appreciate her advocacy.

We would like to thank Alan Wieder and Craig Kridel for being enthusiastic advocates of the Center and of our work together there. They are both joyful and thoughtful colleagues.

We also appreciate the helpful feedback we received from the anonymous manuscript reviewers and hope our revisions reflect their recommendations. We are especially grateful for the perceptive comments Ray Levi made on earlier drafts. His advice made a huge difference. We are also thankful for the support and advice we have received from Kurt Austin at NCTE. Finally, we want to acknowledge Bonny Graham for the exquisite editing of this book.

Tim is grateful for the many students and families who have helped him grow as a teacher and person. He treasures the relationships he has developed with Center families and the lessons he has learned by working with their children.

Heidi would like to acknowledge her South Carolina Reading Initiative colleagues. Her SCRI literacy coaches and state department liaison served as her primary audience as she wrote Chapter 2, "Daily Life in the Classroom." Heidi's literacy coaches helped her better understand and respond to classroom teachers' needs and interests. Their stories, questions, and perceptive comments, as well as the community they built in their cohort, helped Heidi decide on the content and form for the chapter. Each coach made a unique contribution to Heidi's growth and life for three years. She is grateful to them all: Susan Amick, Clavis Anderson, Diane Dunham, Tamra Gacek, Paula Huggins, Cathy Jones, Michelle Kimpson, Jeannie Knight, Susan Kohler, Carol

Leopold, Lee McDonald, Rose Mitchell, Mamie Shippy, Susan Summer, Rebecca Thomas, Roselyne Thomas, Beth White, Kelly Whitlock, and Clint Wills.

Heidi is just beginning to work with a new cohort of SCRI literacy coaches and looks forward to the chance to live and learn alongside them. She can already tell they are going to share a professionally rich and satisfying journey together over the next several years.

Louise is especially grateful for the ongoing support and encouragement of her husband, Gylton Da Matta, whose insights and experiences regarding diversity, equity, and education inspire her thinking. She is also learning a great deal about the natural capacity of children to inquire from their delightful toddling son, Alex.

Heidi and Tim would like to thank their children, Devin and Colin, for showing them what life is all about. Nothing compares to the love they share with their boys.

Tim would like to thank his mother, RuthAnne O'Keefe Engdal, for inspiring him to become a teacher and for taking a sincere interest in his classroom stories, struggles, and successes.

Finally, we appreciate financial support from a National Council of Teachers of English Grant-in-Aid and a Spencer Foundation Small Grant. This work was also supported in part by a National Academy of Education/Spencer Foundation Postdoctoral Research Fellowship.

1 Exploring Literacy Learning in Inquiry-Based Classrooms

In *Looking Closely* (Mills, O'Keefe, & Stephens, 1992), we attempted to portray the richly complex and embedded nature of literacy learning in a classroom environment that used reading-writing workshop and integrated focus studies as organizational devices. We believed that we needed to provide children opportunities to read and write for diverse purposes every day in order to help them become card-carrying members of the literacy club (Smith, 1981). After analyzing video and audiotapes, samples of children's work, and Tim's kidwatching notes, we identified the teaching strategies that made a difference as children were learning to read and write. We carefully tracked and described the ways in which children learned about phonics (letter-sound relationships) in the process of engaging in and reflecting on authentic literacy events. We also identified assumptions about the learning process that guided Tim's instructional decision making. As he planned for and evaluated children's growth, he did so with these beliefs about how children learn best in mind. Children learn best:

> when the experiences are open-ended and choices are provided;
>
> when they work together and are encouraged to learn from each other;
>
> when they connect new insights to familiar or functional print;
>
> through demonstration, engagement, and reflection;
>
> when they are encouraged to pose their own questions and test their hypotheses;
>
> when they are provided opportunities to celebrate their insights and growth;
>
> and when teachers function as participants, guides, and learners in their classrooms (Mills, O'Keefe, & Stephens, 1992, p. 63).

After ten years, these basic assumptions still underpin Tim's teaching. He strives to teach in ways that are consistent with how children learn. As a teacher-researcher, Tim contributes to the knowledge base on language and learning and also accesses his colleagues' and distant teachers' ideas to help him see more in his own students and to revise his own practices.

Together, we have found Michael Halliday an influential distant teacher and enduring force in our collaborative research. Halliday's (1975) notion that children have opportunities to learn language, learn about language, and learn through language when involved in genuine literacy events has helped us reflect on the teaching and learning potential in Tim's classroom over time. Tim's teaching is grounded in inquiry (Lindfors, 1999; Smith, 1998). He provides consistently rich opportunities for children to inquire into and learn about reading and writing (i.e., learn the code [phonics], effective strategies for constructing meaning across genres, and writing conventions such as spelling, grammar, and punctuation). His students use language to inquire—simultaneously seeking to understand, explore, act on, critique, and make a difference in the world.

Halliday's model has been such a driving force in Heidi and Tim's thinking and teaching that we consulted it to help us develop a theoretically sound mathematics curriculum. Heidi and Tim had the privilege of engaging in collaborative research with David Whitin for several years. David helped us see the power of Halliday's model in supporting mathematical literacy. During that time, we took the theoretical framework that had guided our work in literacy and transferred it to mathematics because David helped us realize that math is a language too. To better understand our work in mathematical literacy, we recommend *Living and Learning Mathematics: Stories and Strategies for Supporting Mathematical Literacy* (Whitin, Mills, & O'Keefe, 1990) and *Mathematics in the Making: Authoring Ideas in Primary Classrooms* (Mills, O'Keefe, & Whitin, 1996). We also recommend a marvelous new book by David Whitin and Robin Cox titled *A Mathematical Passage: Strategies for Promoting Inquiry in Grades 4–6* (2003).

Halliday's work pushed us to use a curricular framework that encourages children to learn mathematics, learn about mathematics, and learn through mathematics (see Figure 1.1).

In *Looking Closely* (1992), we concentrated on the ways in which the children were learning about language, phonics in particular. We could easily, however, have taken the same classroom data and interpreted it by focusing on the ways in which children were learning language, learning about language, and also using language as a tool for learning. We know it's the lens we use to examine our students that ultimately determines what we see. One of our favorite vignettes in *Looking Closely* is titled "Mathematics: Playground Stories." Given the

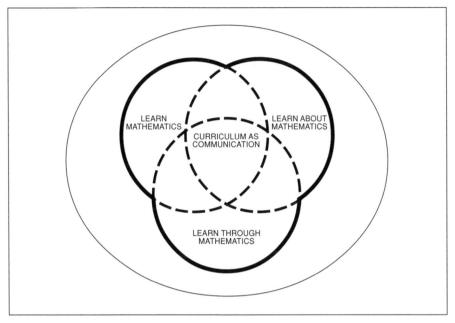

Figure 1.1. Model of mathematical literacy.

richness of the engagements, the teaching and learning potential of the same texts can be interpreted by uncovering the ways in which the children were learning language, learning about language, and learning through language.

Mathematical Playground Stories

In this vignette, Tim invited Kareem to share with the whole class a survey Kareem had conducted the day before. Kareem's survey had grown out of an intense interest in playground activities because a new walking and running path around the school property had just been completed. Kareem asked his friends, "Do you like football or swings or Frisbee? You can sign up for two." As Kareem shared his survey, Tim responded, "Why did you let people pick two?"

"'Cause they would probably like it," was Kareem's matter-of-fact response.

After some conversation, it was determined that Kareem's survey revealed certain information about his inquiry but left many questions unanswered. Several children contested his results by arguing that their favorite playground activities were not listed. Tim took notes during the conversation and seized the opportunity to help them become

Figure 1.2. Amanda's visual representation of Tim's survey results.

better consumers of mathematical data. He devised a plan to demonstrate how the questions we ask influence what we find.

The next day Tim conducted his own survey as children entered the classroom. He told them that he liked Kareem's idea so much that he wanted to build on it. His survey was also about playground activities but his question was open-ended. He asked, "What is your favorite thing to do on the playground?"

Tim wrote their responses next to their names and then looked for patterns in the data. He noticed that seven children chose Frisbee, two identified jumping rope, two liked the swings, one liked the monkey bars, one liked kickball, one preferred football, one liked walking, and three said they liked running on the new trail best. Tim asked Amanda to help him create a visual representation of the patterns he had identified using the mathematical data (see Figure 1.2).

After sharing the visual and discussing it at their morning meeting, Tim reminded the students of the importance of being skeptical consumers of mathematical data. He validated both surveys and said they revealed a lot of important information. He reminded them, however, to think about the question or the meaning underlying the numerals. They discussed a number of different questions they could ask on

Figure 1.3. Tony's visual representation of the mathematical equation 5 + 1 = 6.

playground surveys and how each question would influence the answers they would ultimately get.

Next, Tim capitalized on their interest in playground activities by inviting the class to engage in some mathematical problem posing and solving. He distributed class photos and asked the children to create their own playground stories using art, mathematics, and writing. They looked at the photos, thought about whom they played with and what they did most frequently, and then composed their own playground texts. The children all created novel and interesting mathematical stories. Tony sketched five children and one adult and created the equation $5 + 1 = 6$ to represent the event mathematically. Next he wrote: "Mr. O'Keefe threw the frisbee and I caught it. Justin jumped up. Derrick was too small. I was blocking Derrick" (see Figure 1.3). They published these stories by reading them aloud to their classmates and teacher.

Reflecting on the Playground Stories

This mini-inquiry project revealed the ways in which the children were provided opportunities to learn language, learn about language, and learn through language, including learning to critique through language (Egawa & Harste, 2001). These two primary engagements, the playground surveys and playground stories, provided opportunities for the six-year-olds to further experience the processes involved in *learning oral and written language*. The surveys and discussion promoted oral language growth as the children discussed the problems and possibilities as a classroom community. The conversation gave them the chance to pose questions, share their own ideas, tell their own stories, and defend their positions (Lindfors, 1999). The more children talk to learn, the more they learn how to talk well. The playground stories gave children a chance to shape a common personal experience into story form. And it is our capacity to create and share stories that makes us uniquely human. As Rosen (1985) and Wells (1986) argue, we shape our experiences into story form first to understand and then to share our understanding with others. These children were learning and using the power of story to understand and communicate.

The playground stories encouraged the children to *learn about language* by providing opportunities to use what they currently knew about spelling, grammar, and punctuation, as well as the complementary relationship between illustrations and texts in well-written stories. Tony revealed his resourcefulness in his piece; he knew how to access familiar print to spell words conventionally, such as his teacher's name. He demonstrated this as he left his table, walked over to his teacher's desk and copied Mr. O'Keefe's name, and then found a Frisbee in the closet to borrow its conventional spelling. He spelled high-frequency words such as *the, up,* and *and* conventionally and used what he knew about phonics to invent spellings for unknown words. Given the inconsistencies in the English written language, Tony's spelling strategies were logical, systematic, and rule governed (Dahl, Scharer, Lawson, & Grogan, 2001). They made sense given his previous encounters with print and his developing understanding of letter-sound relationships. Another important aspect of this engagement is that it provided Tim with important information about Tony's use of onsets (the first part of syllables) and rimes (the last part of syllables) (Moustafa, 1997). Later, Tim used such kidwatching data to make instructional decisions during spelling/word study minilessons (Harwayne, 2001).

The playground stories gave the children a chance to *learn through language* as they collected and analyzed mathematical data to write a short, nonfiction piece. They learned how to gather information for their stories, and they learned how to write stories that helped them better appreciate the passions and relationships inherent in their classroom community. Their stories portrayed unique friendships and their classmates' special athletic interests and strengths. Additionally, they learned more about one another as friends and authors as they published their playground stories.

The children in this transition first-grade classroom were given the opportunity to learn to critique through language as well (Cambourne, 2003). Tim capitalized on the conversation that emerged from Kareem's original survey to explicitly address common misconceptions and misinterpretations in survey research. Our culture often blindly accepts numerical data from graphs and surveys as fact or truth. Tim helped these young children become more sophisticated members of our democracy by teaching them about the relationship between the questions we ask and the answers we find. After Kareem's introduction to this concept, Tim invited the children to bring in graph and survey information from *USA Today* and *The State* newspapers. These sources allowed them to further explore the problems as well as possibilities inherent in the ways we construct and publicly share information. The students also discussed the importance of asking questions as consumers of language and mathematical literacy. They were learning the importance of inquiry in our democracy.

Structures and Strategies That Support Literacy

As we strive to better support readers and writers, we realize that strategy lesson instruction is at the heart of our work. Strategy lessons allow us to highlight some aspect of literacy for which students need support within the context of authentic reading and writing events (Short & Harste, 1996). Strategy lessons illuminate features or functions of language while keeping all of the cueing systems intact and working in concert. They also encourage readers and writers to reflect on and become conscious of the processes involved in reading and writing so that they can learn to orchestrate cueing systems strategically. Accomplished teachers such as Tim pay careful attention to children's strengths and needs and then create experiences that highlight an aspect of language for which the students need support. They access or devise strategy lessons because they believe that children learn best when they attend to skills and strategies as they occur in authentic literacy events.

As students engage in strategy lessons, they are provided genuine opportunities to learn language, learn about language, and learn through language (Halliday, 1975). Although all three aspects of literacy learning are inherent in all literacy engagements, children and/or teachers often highlight one of them for special attention (Rowe, 1986). It is important to note that strategy lessons illuminate a feature of language without isolating it from its use. Therefore, children learn the value of the skill or strategy by exploring its role in natural literacy contexts.

Strategy lessons that promote language learning are those that focus on the "doing" of language—reading, writing, speaking, and listening. *Learning language* involves learning how to use oral and written language in one's social world to meet one's particular purposes and intentions. Children gain insights into the functions and purposes of language by speaking, listening, reading, and writing. Tim immerses his learners in opportunities to engage in rich, diverse, and meaningful literacy experiences day in and day out. He does so by making space in the daily schedule for literacy structures such as read-alouds and independent reading and writing time (Allington, 2001; Hahn, 2002).

Children *learn about language* as they explore its various functions and conventions as a communication system. As children reflect on how language is constructed and used in various contexts, they develop and fine-tune their capacity to use language conventions to communicate effectively. They learn the functions of the conventions and explore ways to use them to give their own reading and writing power (Hindley, 1996; Ray, 1999). Tim helps his students learn about language through minilessons, strategy lessons, shared reading, reading and writing conferences, author studies, and genre and craft studies.

Children *learn through language* as they use reading, writing, and talking to explore and expand their understanding of the world. Children learn content knowledge as well as procedural knowledge when using oral and written language as tools for learning. Through language and literature-based engagements, children learn to reflect on what they are learning and generate new thoughts. Tim helps his students learn through language as they engage in literature study, writing workshop, focus studies, math workshop, and various class journals. His students use tools such as literature response journals, writer's notebooks, and learning logs to capture, interpret, and share new insights and ideas.

According to Short, "As teachers, our goal is to make sure that students are involved in learning events that center around each of these three opportunities" (1997, p.32). Building on recommendations from Short and Halliday (1975), Tim has created a curricular framework that includes literacy structures such as read-aloud, shared reading, literature study groups, writing workshop, and focus studies that connect to the daily life of the classroom. By doing so, he provides daily opportunities for children to learn literacy, learn about literacy, and learn through literacy (see Figure 1.4, adapted from Short [1997]). While each literacy structure has the potential to help children learn language, learn about

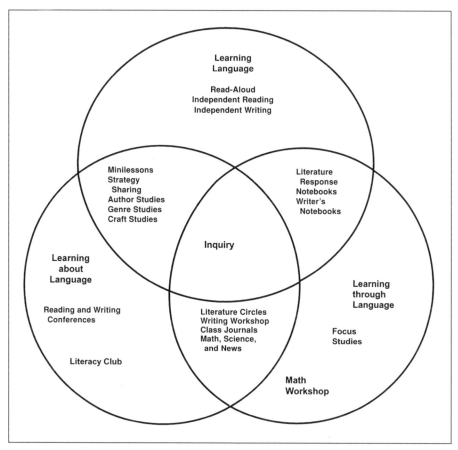

Figure 1.4. Curricular framework encompassing learning language, learning about language, and learning through language.

language, and learn through language, each plays a unique role in the curriculum. (We recommend *Literature as a Way of Knowing* by Kathy Short [1997] for further inquiry into the relationship between various literacy structures and the opportunities they provide children to learn, learn about, and learn through language.)

Shared reading provides opportunities for children to learn what effective/strategic readers do and how the reading process works in the context of a large group, with the teacher demonstrating and orchestrating the process. Tim invites his students to participate by reading along and responding to reading strategy prompts within the security of a large group.

Reading conferences offer Tim and his students opportunities to learn and apply reading strategies in an intimate setting. Tim uses a modified version of miscue analysis, interviews, self-assessments, and kidwatching notes to gain insight into children's strengths, needs, and interests as readers. Reading conferences provide Tim and his students the chance to hold conversations about the reading process and content of the book.

Literature study groups provide opportunities for children to hold "grand conversations" about books they choose (Peterson & Eeds, 1990; Smith, 1998). They encourage children to make text-to-text, text-to-self, and text-to-world connections (Keene & Zimmermann, 1997). Consequently, children learn the value of responding to literature both aesthetically and efferently (Rosenblatt, 1995). They learn about language through author studies, genre studies, and craft studies. Through rich conversations about high-quality literature, children learn that literature can be both informative and transformative.

Writing workshop provides opportunities for Tim and his students to compose, revise, edit, and publish through the authoring cycle model. They learn to think, work, and communicate as authors by engaging in craft, skill, and strategy lessons (Fletcher & Portalupi, 2001; Ray, 2002). They learn the power of choice, ownership, and voice in writing. They also learn to write while employing writing as a tool for learning about themselves and the world. In Short and Harste's words, "The generative aspect of writing is what we call learning" (1996, p. 32).

The Rest of The Story

As we share stories and strategies from Tim's second- and third-grade classrooms throughout the rest of this book, we will do so in several different ways. In this introduction, we intentionally chose to tease out the ways in which children are provided opportunities to learn language, learn about language, and learn through language. While this theoretical framework will continue to serve as the anchor and springboard for the stories to come, it will be contextualized within a description of a typical day so that readers can come to appreciate the curricular structures and patterns of daily life in his classroom that make a difference. The framework also will be used as a lens through which to reveal patterns of growth and change in two students over a two-year period. And it will function as the touchstone for describing the ways in which Tim builds a democratic classroom community and the way in which he communicates with parents.

As each chapter addresses different dimensions of Tim's teaching, we hope it will become clear that different literacy engagements foreground different learning opportunities. There are times in Tim's classroom each day when he intentionally and systematically conducts minilessons or reflective strategy sharing sessions to *teach children about language.* While he does so in the process of authentic literacy engagements, he clearly helps students appreciate, learn, and use language conventions such as spelling, grammar, and punctuation. He also helps them appreciate, learn, and use all cueing systems (graphophonemic, syntactic, and semantic) in concert. In other words, his students become strategic readers by balancing all cueing systems as they read.

It becomes clear at other times each day that Tim has planned in ways that encourage children to *learn through language.* His second and third graders read and write for a variety of purposes every day. And some of the most compelling literacy experiences take place as children are investigating a physical or social science concept. Reading and writing are central tools for learning across the day and the year regardless of the unit of study.

Of course, children continue *learning language* all day, every day through authentic opportunities to read, write, and talk together.

2 Daily Life in the Classroom

Tim realizes the importance and power of perceptive kidwatching (Goodman, 1978; O'Keefe, 1997). He knows his students well. He knows the strategies they use when constructing meaning through print. He knows their favorite authors. He knows the genres they choose to read and write. He knows how they make connections, the kinds of questions they pose, the things that capture their hearts and minds. He knows their habits, passions, and fears. He knows he has to know these things and so he devotes time and attention to these matters. He knows he has to know his kids first.

We have learned, however, that knowing kids is necessary but not sufficient. Teaching is complex. It involves orchestrating multiple data sources simultaneously. Accomplished teachers intentionally tap into district and state standards and utilize instructional materials as potential teaching resources. Yet they do so much more. They don't simply teach the standards or the texts. In fact, they don't simply teach reading and writing. Good teachers teach *readers and writers.* They do so by teaching responsively. Teachers who pay careful attention to their students' strengths and needs can respond in ways that make a difference moment by moment, child to child, day in and day out. Teachers who understand the literacy learning process and make a habit of collecting kidwatching data on children are in the best position to strategically teach and reach readers and writers. Decisions they make are grounded in a solid professional knowledge base that comes to life when teachers, texts, and kids come together.

We have also learned that having a professional knowledge base is necessary but not sufficient. We need a solid framework in which to teach and learn. As humans, we thrive within predictable structures. We find comfort in the routines and rituals that make up our lives (Peterson, 1992). We find special satisfaction when the routines and rituals foster community and provide the kind of open-ended support that promotes growth and change. So it is with children in the classroom. It is important for them to know they can count on time to read independently; time to read together and talk about what they are reading; time to work on a piece that is theirs alone; time to read, write, and talk about the daily news or a focused study project. Curricular structures such as read-aloud, literature study, writing workshop, math workshop, and focused studies give the teacher and children the time, space, and support necessary to learn language, learn about language, and learn through language.

This chapter illuminates how one teacher, a teacher who embraces inquiry as a way of knowing and being in the classroom, thinks, plans, and responds to his students throughout each day. Because teachers often say it is hard to put it all together, we weave responses to common questions teachers ask into the text. Teachers frequently wonder how to make instructional decisions; how to best use time; how to strike a healthy balance between the state and district standards and the children's genuine needs and interests; how to teach readers and writers to become more strategic and independent; and how to help children use reading and writing as tools for learning across the curriculum. We show and tell how Tim addresses these issues in the daily life of his classroom. We describe the structures and common teaching practices that make up each segment of his day. Then we share artifacts or classroom vignettes to show what these beliefs and practices look and sound like in Tim's classroom. Basically, we walk you through his day using his current schedule.

Typical Daily Forecast

8:10–8:45	Exploration
8:45–9:30	Morning Meeting
9:30–11:00	Reading Workshop (MWF) and Writing Workshop (TTh)
11:00–12:00	Lunch and Recess
12:00–12:15	Chapter Book Read-Aloud
12:15–1:15	Math Workshop
1:15–2:30	Focused Studies (Science or Social Studies Units of Study)
2:30–2:50	Reflection, Friendship Circle, and Homework

Note that this schedule is merely an outline, a tool used for planning. Very often the actual schedule varies from this—that's why we call it a forecast (Gilbert, personal communication, October 2000). A morning meeting may last longer than planned if a large number of children have contributed to class journals or if something important has happened in the news. Workshop time may resume after lunch if too many children had pieces to publish in the morning. Structures are created to provide predictability and support. It is equally important, however, to modify them when necessary in order to teach responsively. If the schedule truly supports learning and learners, it is written in pencil and revised when necessary (Burke, 1996).

EXPLORATION: 8:10–8:45

Getting Started: The Importance of Feeling Welcome

Tim wants his students to feel welcome, smart, and valued each and every day. He wants them to look forward to the time they will spend together and to leave the classroom each day with a feeling of accomplishment and with interesting stories to tell their family and friends. He knows that some children will enter his room feeling competent and confident, while others will be hesitant and less experienced as readers, writers, mathematicians, or scientists. So he does what he has to do. Through his actions, he "believes" them into being thoughtful, caring, and competent members of his classroom community. This isn't always an easy stance to take. But we know that the messages we send kids about them will greatly influence the classroom community. We have come to believe that all voices, soft and loud, must be heard, respected, and valued in healthy learning communities. Strong classroom communities promote collaboration, which in turn enhances academic rigor, independence, confidence, and competence. So Tim makes time and space at the beginning of the day for exploration, a time for kids to pursue areas of personal interest and a time for intimate bonding.

Regie Routman confirms the importance of bonding in *Reading Essentials* (2003b). She puts it this way:

> Curriculum and standards must first connect with the lives and spirits of our children if we're going to have any lasting success. Unless we reach into our students' hearts, we have no entry into their minds. . . . Bonding with our students is the "human essential," the intimately personal connection that is the core of responsive, excellent teaching. (p.12)

So Tim and the children begin each day with an exploration period, a period that gives the kids a chance to work in areas of their personal interest and to bond with their teacher and one another. It is a relaxed time of day when stories are told and hugs are given. During this time, children also continue learning language through immersion in reading, writing, and talking.

The children cross the threshold into the classroom around 8:10 a.m. Between 8:10 and 8:45, they spend time casually chatting while hanging up their book bags and/or turning in their homework projects. During this time, children may read independently or together, work on pieces they are preparing for publication, play chess or commercial games, make observations in the science area, read the local newspaper, write observations or questions about a class science, math, language, or news journal, and so on. Tim makes a point of personally connecting with each child. He also takes advantage of this time to make observations about how the kids choose to use independent work time. He makes notes of the areas in the classroom that are accessed most and the ways in which children work together. He usually selects a light jazz, classical, or instrumental piece for background music. While the choices do vary, this list represents common choices made during exploration time (see Figure 2.1).

How Exploration Time Looks and Sounds

Soft music is playing in the background as the children begin their settling-in activities. Usually Tim selects a CD for background music. On this particular day, the music is not coming from the tape player but instead from the teacher and three children who are helping him compose a tune on guitar for their class song. These three children have coauthored the words, and they are advising the teacher on the tune they have in mind for their poetic text titled "People of the World." Jack is reading a book to help him understand why water has stronger surface tension than alcohol. Elijah is working on his battery and bulb project. Laura is writing an entry in the class language journal. Victoria is immersed in a chapter book and successfully ignoring most of the activity around her. Sarah is putting the finishing touches on a piece she is preparing for publication. Mahogany and Courtney are playing chess with Mrs. McPheters, the Master of Arts in Teaching (MAT) intern (student teacher from USC). Several children are playing math games together on the floor. Jonathon is working on a switch for his electricity investigation. After Tim spends five minutes or so with the songwriting group, he walks around the room to touch base with each child and/or group. The room is humming in a comfortable, focused, and productive way.

MORNING MEETING: 8:45–9:30

Tim signals the end of exploration time and the transition to morning meeting with music. He and the children select songs to signify cleanup time. They use songs such as "Put a Little Love in Your Life" by Del

Figure 2.1. During exploration time, Tim's students engage in a variety of activities.

Shannon to inspire them to sing along while cleaning up the classroom and moving to the carpet in the front of the room. Tim has found that the intimacy of children gathered together on the floor helps them focus and tune in to the conversation. They can easily see and hear one another and the texts being explored.

Morning meetings foster community building as well as exploratory conversations. In Tim's room, the morning meeting is one of the richest and most intellectually rigorous times in his daily schedule. In fact, the morning meeting demonstrates the essence of an inquiry-based curriculum. Tim strives to make it a time when children make connections between the content they have been exploring in school and their personal lives. They look for connections between work at school and the world. They also use this time to institute the processes and adopt the multiple perspectives that are at the heart of inquiry. In other words, this time of day is central to curricular integration. They take all the skills, concepts, content, and strategies and make them their own. When Brenda Miller Power visited his Tim's classroom in 1998, she wrote, "I thought Tim O'Keefe's morning meeting was amazing . . . such a wide-ranging, thoughtful exploration of current events, math, science, and music. He sets high standards for the kids academically and socially, yet he still creates a very natural environment."

A number of academic rituals are part of typical morning meetings in this class. Kids start preparing for the meeting before coming together on the carpet. Tim puts out large class journals during exploration time. These journals are simply large blank books made from construction paper. The children are encouraged to make observations and pose questions as mathematicians, scientists, readers, and authors. They then bring the science, math, and language journals to the meeting for conversation. They also look through the newspaper to bring current events into the conversation by sharing articles that spark their interest as young historians. They put their clippings in the class news journal or hang them on the news bulletin board. Tim participates in the process alongside the children, making interesting, careful observations of the world and documenting them in the journals. He shows the kids that being a careful observer of the world is central to learning. He also poses authentic questions that come to mind. The following observations and questions represent the content and nature of Tim's entries in various class journals:

Science Journals

I notice when you look at something with the field microscope, it appears upside down. I wonder why?

I saw the moon this morning about 6:30 a.m. It looked like a C. It was two fists above the horizon.

All of the painted lady butterfly larvae have changed to chrysalises (or chrysalides). You can see the final shed skin in the bottom of the cups or on the chrysalises.

Math Journals

I noticed that we have burned one full candle during our reading time so far this year. It took almost one month. At this rate we would burn about 9 1/2 candles this year (one for every month).

The average person's heart will beat about 2 1/2 billion times in their lifetime. WOW! (2,500,000,000) (2 billion, 500 million)

In reference to a newspaper article about worldwide graduation rates: I wonder why so few U.S teenagers graduate from H.S. compared to other countries (industrialized nations)?

Language Journals

In English when we want to write about someone laughing we write <u>ha ha</u> or something like that. I wonder what they would write for laughter in other languages?

It seems that when I was small there were lots of cars named after animals (Jaguar, Impala, Mustang, even the VW Beetle). I wonder why there aren't many new cars named after animals now?

I noticed the length of two stories in the newspaper on Sunday. We talked about this earlier. Why do some stories get lots of print and others get so little print?

You can imagine how these questions and observations are connected to units of study about large numbers, calculating and interpreting rates in mathematics, cycles in nature, astronomy, social justice, the meaning of and changes in our vocabulary, and so on. You can also imagine how such questions inspire kids to become passionate learners.

The children follow Tim's lead and begin living the life of inquirers by looking at the world as mathematicians, scientists, authors, and historians. They document their insights and wonders in the journals in preparation for the morning meeting conversation (see Figure 2.2). Tim also reminds them to do so throughout the day as they make observations or pose questions. He frequently responds to kids' discussions by recommending that they make an entry in one of the class journals to continue the conversation formally.

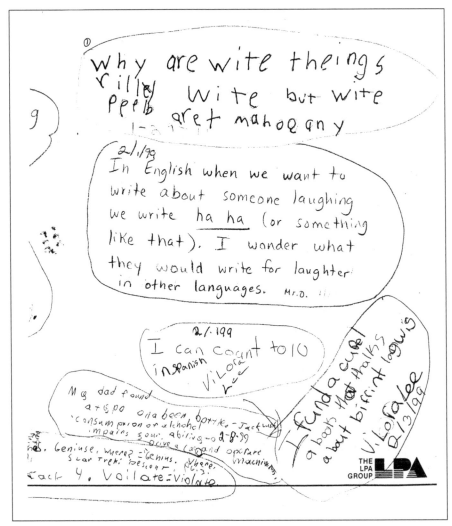

Figure 2.2. A typical page from the class language journal.

The Meeting Begins

Taking Care of Business

Tim opens the meeting by taking attendance and lunch count. A designated child grabs the stopwatch, looks around the room, and, when everyone is poised, begins the clock. Another child reads the names on the class roster. Kids respond by stating "home lunch" or "school lunch."

The timer stops the watch as soon as the last child answers. The child with the stopwatch calls out the time, and the class calculates the difference between today's time and the class record. The children are asked to calculate the difference mentally to the hundredths of a second. Then they check the answer together. Their goal is to continually improve their efficiency. Tim weaves mathematical insights and strategies into the problem each day. This ritual helps them conduct daily business in a timely fashion and engages them in realistic mathematical problem solving. It is also an opportunity to practice a subtraction problem each day involving decimals, often with regrouping.

Next, the students take the number of the day (number of days in school thus far) and respond to the question: *What do you know about this number?* The children challenge themselves and one another to think of facts about the number of the day and diverse equations that could be used to reach the number, as well as personal connections to the numeral, such as a grandmother's age. Then they add and exchange coins by manipulating the money calendar, representing the same number by placing the appropriate pennies, nickels, dimes, quarters, and dollars in clear plastic bags taped across the top of the board. Each day a penny is added and the coins are regrouped to have the fewest coins possible represent the number of the day. Once five pennies are placed in the penny bag, they are removed and exchanged for a nickel. If there are two nickels, they are replaced by a dime, and so on. When all the regrouping has taken place, the class counts the money together. The children's repeated engagements with the process help them internalize strategies for making and counting change. Finally, the class meteorologist reports on the day's temperature, and the students discuss patterns in the weather data they have been collecting over time.

The majority of morning meeting time is devoted to the news and class journals. The children share their observations and questions and call on their friends and teachers to make connections, offer possible explanations, or ask related questions. The conversations reflect Judith Lindfors's notion of using inquiry utterances to learn (1999). They also reflect the fact that Tim willingly shares power with his young apprentices. Lindfors illuminates the value of such a stance this way:

> What are we to make of the teacher's sense that she is giving something up when she takes children's inquiry seriously, even to the extent of making it the fundamental shared expectation in collaborative inquiry genres such as discussion and science talks? What does she lose? I submit that what the teacher is giving up is control but not power. Indeed, in exploratory classroom genres,

the measure of her loss of control may be precisely the measure of her gain in power, for if her goal in such events is to better understand the children's thinking, then the more that the thinking can reveal itself, the more fully she reaches her goal. . . . In collaborative inquiry events such as discussions and science talks, I hear empowered children. I also hear empowered teachers. (p. 174)

The following description of journal sharing time during morning meeting brings Lindfors's ideas to life and shows what genuine inquiry sounds like during this curricular structure. During morning meeting, the children are immersed in demonstrations and engagements that help them learn about their world and themselves through oral and written language. Additionally, the language journal is a tool that offers possibilities for learning about language by allowing children to reflect on its unique forms, structures, and functions.

How Class Journal Sharing Looks and Sounds

Tim initiated the class journal component of morning meeting this day by asking if anyone had brought news from home to share.

Laura held up a section of the newspaper and remarked, "There was a little part at the zoo with a snake as the sidewalk. Here is a picture of the pattern. When we went to the zoo, we bought a brick for my nana." The group nodded because they knew the zoo had been encouraging the purchase of bricks on a pathway as a fund-raising drive.

Dani responded, "Somebody painted a picture like that in art," making a connection between the two experiences.

"Where is that?" a child asked, referring to the location of the bricks at the zoo.

Laura clarified, "It is over the bridge. There are, like, stores there."

Faith made a personal connection, "Sometimes we take a trolley across the zoo. When we get off the bridge, we start seeing the pattern like that."

Tim held up another section of the newspaper and pointed to the section just above the weather forecast. "It is Rosa Parks's birthday. Rosa Parks is a civil rights pioneer and she is eighty-six today. Happy birthday, Rosa."

Courtney asked, "Is Rosa Parks dead yet?"

"No, today she is eighty-six. The people listed in this section of the paper are still living. You wouldn't find George Washington in this section," Tim clarified.

Courtney continued, "Martin Luther King is dead."

Tim said, "Right, but you wouldn't see his birthday listed here in this section of the paper where it says today's birthdays." Tim uses this time to illuminate how newspapers are constructed, in addition to providing a careful examination and exploration of their content.

Tim turned to another story in the paper: "Here is an article about the lynx. I thought Melissa would like this one since she did her report on the lynx. It says that they are going to reintroduce more pairs of lynx to the mountains in the West where they are endangered."

Several kids asked what the lynx looked like and Melissa answered with authority, "They look like a little bobcat."

Tim pushed the conversation on by suggesting that some people are against the reintroduction and asked if they could predict who and why?

A number of children chimed in simultaneously, "Hunters, zoos, poachers."

The conversation continued for a few minutes as children generated hypotheses, revised their ideas, and carefully considered one another's perspectives. Tim referred to the article to help them fine-tune their predictions. He read a section of the article stating that the ranchers fear that the animals may harm their livestock.

The kids reacted, "Oh, farmers." Many of them had that classic "Of course, that makes sense" look on their face.

"I have one more article to share. It's about the fact that our speed limits are about to go up on our interstates in South Carolina. It is also about stopping people who don't wear seat belts. There are two kinds of seat belt laws. One is called primary enforcement, meaning they can stop you if they see you're not wearing a seat belt. This graph shows that in states with primary enforcement, 78 percent of the citizens wear seat belts, and in states like ours with secondary enforcement, only 63 percent of the people wear seat belts." Tim regularly accesses graphs to demonstrate the role of math as a tool for learning. He seeks to help his students understand how to pose questions and collect, organize, and display quantitative data in informative and compelling ways. As he does so, children probe below the surface of the information. They ask questions about methods of data collection and the meaning of the results.

Ali asked, "What about the backseat; how could they tell?"

"That's a good question. Maybe they're just looking at the drivers," Tim answered.

"How did they find that out?" another inquired.

Heidi was videotaping and chimed in, "They could have conducted anonymous surveys."

Tim clarified by saying, "They could have asked a thousand people whether they wear seat belts regularly or not, and they calculated the percentages that reflected their answers." He continued, "We know through statistics that people who wear seat belts are more likely to survive a high-speed accident."

Tim turned the group's attention to the entries they had made in the class journals that morning. Laura said she had something in the language journal, opening it to the page marked by a sticky note. "You know how we have books written in different languages and, like, sign language?"

The class immediately put their fingers together in the shape of the sign they had just learned for *friendship*. Laura nodded, realizing they were with her.

Laura continued, "This book is called *Wolf Talk*. It's about how wolves communicate."

Tim encouraged her to share the book with the class and to write key ideas she had learned from the book in the language journal. The class had been using the language journal to record insights about communication across sign systems and species.

Jack said he had written an observation in the science journal. He opened it and read, "I looked at the piece of bread we wiped on Angelo's shell [the class turtle] to study the growth of bacteria. And it looked like this [pointing to his sketch in the journal]. The brown is the bread and the green splotches are the bacteria."

Tim added, "We moistened the bread and wiped it on different things around the room, and the only thing growing was from our turtle's shell. It has a lot of things growing on it." He continued, "Don't open these bags, boys and girls," reminding them of the health hazards of a mistake in this kind of scientific research.

Tim mentioned that he had something in the science journal as well. They had previously discussed optical illusions when the pilot who crashed into a ski resort in Italy claimed it was because of an optical illusion. Tim opened the science journal and pointed to a sketch: "Here is an optical illusion I know how to draw. Jack called it a dimension door and Victoria called it an artist's trick." The children leaned in to take a closer look. "Cool!" was a common response that signified their amazement.

Before closing the conversation, Tim took care of class business by suggesting, "Since we are finished with our lightbulb projects, let's take them apart today but keep the diagrams to put in your science portfolios. They demonstrate a lot of what you have learned about electricity and circuits."

Just then, Victoria remembered she had an entry in the language journal that she had forgotten to share. "I have something in the language journal. In this book I got at the book fair, I was reading it and on page 11 I thought I found a typo but it wasn't. I thought at the end of every sentence you had to put a quotation mark, but I found out that if the same person is saying it, you can just put it [meaning a quotation mark] at the beginning and end of the whole thing," she said, displaying the text.

Tim pointed to her text and added, "There's Baby Dill. And since Baby Dill is the only one talking, there is one passage. That's a good one. And that is a great reminder for writing workshop. When you are using dialogue, try to remember to use quotation marks appropriately."

Tim has found that these incidental moments that emerge every day are invaluable opportunities to revisit the skills, strategies, and content the students address during reading, writing, science, and math workshop. This particular morning meeting demonstrates the structures or common rituals that Tim has established in his classroom. While the rituals remain consistent over time, the ebb and flow as well as the passion of the conversations vary.

READING OR WRITING WORKSHOP: 9:30–11:00

(Reading Workshop on Monday, Wednesday, and Friday;
Writing Workshop on Tuesday and Thursday)

Over the years, Tim has created large blocks of uninterrupted time for reading or writing workshop. He has found it much more effective to hold reading workshop on Monday, Wednesday, and Friday and writing workshop on Tuesday and Thursday than to rush kids through both structures each day. Of course, kids write during reading workshop and read during writing workshop.

The reading process and the skills and strategies involved in it are foregrounded during reading workshop. The writing process, with craft lessons as well as the skills and strategies good writers use, are featured during writing workshop. Consequently, each workshop has unique yet theoretically congruent features. Tim does not claim to own or to have discovered the perfect structures for his workshops, and he has changed them over the years. We are simply sharing what works for him at this moment in time. It is our hope that you will use what has the potential to work for you in light of your professional reading and personal teaching experiences. Each workshop provides daily opportunities for children to learn language by engaging in the process as readers or writers; learn about language by reflecting on and analyzing its structures, forms, and functions; and learn through language by using it as a tool for learning and expressing their ideas and current understandings.

Reading Workshop

Read-Alouds

Reading workshop involves read-alouds, independent reading, reading conferences, and literature study groups. Read-alouds are central to Tim's teaching. He often chooses picture books from an author study or text set of related books for daily read-alouds. Since read-alouds often function as the anchor as well as the springboard for the curriculum, Tim selects books carefully. He chooses high-quality literature that inspires kids to appreciate the craft of writing and the power of language. He exposes children to magnificent authors such as Arnold Adoff, Avi, Byrd Baylor, Eve Bunting, Sharon Creech, Tomie dePaola, Ralph Fletcher, Mem Fox, Jean Craighead George, Gloria Houston, Thomas Locker, Patricia MacLachlan, Walter Dean Meyers, Patricia Polacco, Chris Van Allsburg, E. B. White, and Douglas Wood. He also reads chapter books from well-known series such as The Wizard of Oz and Shiloh. He also selects books that communicate messages about content that connect to unifying concepts that frame the curriculum, such as cycles, change, or systems, or to particular units of study, such as civil rights, electricity, botany, or South Carolina history.

Tim wants the children to adopt a "reading as inquiry" stance, so he uses read-aloud time to think out loud, to pose questions in the midst and after the fact, to shift perspective, and to show what critical, strategic readers do. Since the children often adopt the teacher's model of literacy (DeFord, 1981), we believe it is crucial to make inquiry visible and explicit. We have found that the children begin thinking and talking like their teachers soon after school begins. So read-aloud time helps kids appreciate the beauty and power of good books as well as the ways readers might interact with texts (Rosenblatt, 1995).

Read-alouds also serve as invitations for children to create their own written pieces when inspired by a particular author or series. Written reflections on read-alouds are the foundation for writing in another way as well. They are simply sources of story—a repertoire of story experiences from which to draw on when reading and writing.

Although the children often hold grand conversations after Tim completes the reading (Peterson & Eeds, 1990), he frequently invites them to sketch or write a response in their literature response journals before embarking on a whole-class conversation. He has found that the conversations are often richer if kids have a chance to think deeply about the text before sharing with others. We have found that it is important to explicitly demonstrate a range of literature response options (sketch to stretch, written conversation, poetry, letters, freewrite narratives, lists, etc.) and give them multiple chances to practice them. But we have also learned that it is critical to allow kids to begin making choices about literature response strategies *they want to use* as soon as possible.

Literature responses often help children think about what they want to offer in the conversation before it begins. This in turn helps promote equity and democracy in the classroom. This process also prepares kids to conduct literature circle conversations in small groups without constant support and direction from the teacher. Basically, Tim uses read-aloud time to help kids learn how to talk about books and how to talk to one another.

Independent Reading and Reading Conferences

The children are given time to read materials of their choice during independent reading. Tim has an extensive classroom library from which they access books; they also take trips to the local library and bring books from home. Kids often select books to read during independent reading time based on recommendations from their friends or their teacher; based on a current and popular children's book series such as the Magic Tree House or Junie B. Jones; or based on an author who was featured during a class author study, such as Chris Van Allsburg or Patricia Polacco.

Although Tim recognizes the value of using this time to practice reading books that match the students' independent reading levels, he does not engage in formulaic matching or limiting children if they have a legitimate reason or desire to read a book that might be a stretch. We have come to understand that children are most strategic as readers when they read with 95 percent accuracy (Allington, 2001; Routman, 2003b). Being strategic means they use reading strategies that reflect the balance of all three cueing systems (semantics, syntax, and grapho-phonemics) efficiently and effectively. But twenty-three years of teaching readers have also taught Tim that while he must make instructional decisions based on a solid research base, he must also remain open to following the kids' lead and his own insights. While a significant body of research promotes the value of matching kids with texts, Tim also believes it was the Harry Potter series and kids' desire to become card-carrying members of the "I'm reading Harry Potter club" that made a critical difference recently for several of his students. They pushed themselves to read the Harry Potter series and truly outgrew themselves in the process. This has been true for many other series as well, including The Wizard of Oz and Shiloh, as well as for individual books such as *Babe: The Gallant Pig*. So Tim urges kids to make wise choices and monitors their selections, but he does so carefully in order not to restrict their access to books and authors they love.

Tim does make suggestions based on what he knows about children as readers, and the whole class engages in many conversations about how to choose good books as well. When kids consistently choose texts that are too easy or too difficult, he does ask them to make a different choice. For the most part, the kids make wise choices and they read materials they have self-selected during independent reading time.

Coaching Readers through Reading Conferences

Tim conducts individual reading conferences with children during independent reading time. This is a calm, quiet time in the room, and Tim finds he can give his students uninterrupted individual attention. He has established a ritual he calls "coaching" for this time, and he keeps an audiotape for each child and a section devoted to coaching readers in his kidwatching notes. He asks the children to bring a book they are currently reading and to select a passage to read aloud, and he sits close enough to see the text. The children know Tim will write while they are reading so they don't let his note taking disrupt them. He invites them to read and then takes notes based on his personalized version of miscue analysis (O'Keefe, 1997) while taping the reading session. Tim's notes focus primarily on the children's use of semantics (meaning), syntax (grammar), and graphophonemics (letter-sound relationships). He looks for patterns in his notes so that he can give children direct feedback in the form of strategy instruction. Before he does so, he often rewinds the tape and invites the child to listen and read along in the story. Next, he asks the child to share what she or he noticed about herself or himself as a reader. Tim takes notes during this reflective talk as well.

We have come to realize that it is as important to capture children's perceptions of themselves as readers as it is to capture what they actually do when engaged with texts. Finally, Tim shares his observations with the child and offers advice in the form of strategy instruction.

Several times during the year, Tim asks each child in the class to read the same story to him during coaching. This allows him to assess the group's capacity to read grade-level materials. Both sets of data (individual selections and the same-text reading) reveal important patterns that help him make instructional decisions for individuals, small groups, and the class as a whole.

How Reading Conferences Look and Sound

Seven-year-old Victoria sat down in the chair next to her teacher and said she was reading Judy Blume's book *Freckle Juice*. Tim asked her to read a new passage to him, and he leaned toward Victoria, listening carefully. On the table, he had paper on a clipboard, and as Victoria read, Tim made occasional notes to record his observations. He also placed a tape recorder on the table and turned it on to capture her reading of this text. As Victoria finished reading, Tim suggested they rewind and replay the end of the tape. Because Tim has learned over time how important it is to invite the reader to share reflections on the reading experience before offering his own, after he and Victoria listened to the tape for a few minutes, his first question to Victoria was, "What do you notice about yourself as a reader?"

Victoria responded, "I notice that I have a little problem with contractions."

"That's interesting. I hadn't written that down. Tell me more about that."

Victoria explained that contractions are two words that come together and how that often confuses her. She added, "My reading was better at the end than it was at the beginning. I didn't miss as many words at the end."

Tim said that he had also noticed that she became more fluent toward the end of the passage. Tim validated Victoria by suggesting that rereading seems to be an effective strategy for her, one that enhanced her fluency.

Next, Victoria and Tim spent a few minutes talking about the value of rereading and how their stances sometimes shift when they do, such as paying more attention to different characters the second time. Tim gave examples of how this is true for him as a reader as well. They talked briefly about how they attended to the characters in *Charlotte's*

Web after reading it or listening to the text read aloud a couple of times. Victoria took the lead in the conversation a couple of times by asking Tim about certain characters in the text.

Tim then asked Victoria what she does when she comes to something she doesn't know in a text. Victoria answered by describing how she looks at word parts and sounds them out. Tim nodded in agreement and then, referring to his notes, began to tell Victoria about the other strategies he noticed she used; for example, she made connections to an earlier passage she had read. She also reread a word or passage when something didn't make sense and self-corrected the miscue. Tim observed that all of these strategies helped Victoria make sense of the story.

Victoria smiled shyly, as if she felt complimented by Tim's observations of her as a reader. Tim smiled inside, hoping he had helped her become more aware of the diverse strategies she used as a reader. Victoria, like many children, needed her strategies to be named and validated. Tim wanted her to become more aware of reading strategies so that she could use them intentionally and flexibly in the future.

Strategy Sharing following Independent Reading

Like most teachers and researchers in literacy education, we have come to appreciate the value of strategy-based instruction. Tim teaches for strategies throughout the day, such as during formal minilessons, when he is coaching individual readers, and when it makes sense in the midst of learning engagements that involve reading and writing. He uses kidwatching data to help him understand patterns in children's strategy use and creates the conditions from which to introduce strategies and try them out. While *strategy instruction* makes a difference, it is the *strategy sharing* time that helps the kids make the strategies their own. Once they own them and share them with others, they internalize their use and value. It is then, we have noticed, that they use them strategically.

Tim builds strategy sharing time into the daily schedule. This predictable ritual gives the children a chance to reflect on the strategies they use and to share them with the class. It gives Tim the opportunity to consider the children's perceptions of the strategies they use and to make explicit the strategies they use implicitly or independently. They name and describe reading strategies and in so doing go public with their thinking. Individual insights become part of the class thought collective. Tim validates, refines, and sometimes extends their thinking as he responds. Thus, children continue learning about language and about the strategies that good readers use.

How Strategy Sharing Looks and Sounds

It was strategy sharing time. The kids all knew what to do. If they had a strategy to share, they volunteered to do so during this academic ritual. Phillip raised his hand. Tim nodded, and Phillip walked to the front of the carpet. All of his young colleagues were gathered together on the floor in front of him. Phillip waited for their attention and then began: "I've got a, let's say there's a word in the sentence that I don't know, like let's say *photosynthesis*. But I do know that word; I know how it looks and how to spell it. But I can use that word for an example. It's like [lifting his hands in front of him and then pointing in the air] it's like, okay, okay, what's that word? Okay [pointing to a word in the air], I'll come back to you. 'Blank is where the sun makes life for plants.' And then that [pointing to the right of the initial spot in the air] gives me a clue. 'Cause I can remember my dad telling me that word is *photosynthesis*. I use the words around it to help me figure it out. And besides, that is also connected to writing. If you know how to read better, you can write better because you've read those words."

Tim responded, "No kidding. The better writer you are, the better reader you are. The better reader you are, the better writer you are. Good connection."

The strategy of using context to assist in meaningful predictions about texts was revisited often during the year. But these informal, often spontaneous examples keep important meaning-based strategies in the front of everyone's mind.

Literature Circles: Talking about Books

Everything comes together during literature circles, or literature study groups. The children employ the strategies they have learned during read-alouds and the written responses and conversations that follow, strategies they practice during independent reading and then refine through reading conferences. Most important, the children have the chance to engage in book talks like those adults hold. We have learned to critique literature study groups by asking if they reflect the passion, interest, and commitment we find in adult book clubs. Although a vision for such a standard is central to inquiry, it is a lot easier imagined than achieved. As Harste (2000) suggests, "It is a lot harder to make a classroom sound holistic than it is to make it look holistic."

Yes, we must make multiple copies of high-quality literature available and help kids work through roles and responsibilities for everyone involved in the literature circle. We have learned, however, the value of carefully orchestrating the transition from read-aloud conversations to small-group literature circles. Many teachers have struggled with literature circles because they focus solely on roles before giving kids first-hand experiences with high-quality conversations in response to read-alouds. We have found that literature circles go well when a solid foundation has been established; for Tim, the foundational concepts are how to talk about books and how to talk with one another. Once these features of the curriculum are firmly in place, the specific roles, responsibilities, and structures that evolve can nurture the conversation rather than dominate it.

We have found the following framework to be central to the establishment of successful literature circles:

1. *Begin with the talk in the classroom.* We want the conversations to reflect the passion, interest, and commitment we find in adult reading guilds. Use read-aloud time to help kids learn how to talk about books and how to talk with one another.

2. *Employ instructional strategies that demonstrate ways to respond to texts.* Intentional, thoughtful instruction occurs within the context of authentic literacy engagements.

3. *Create predictable structures that will help children take hold of the conversation and access response strategies.* Move from whole-group to small-group literature conversations carefully so that children learn to invest in and take ownership of the process (reading, talking, recording insights, questioning, etc., as well as record keeping and self-evaluation strategies). Roles and responsibilities are not the focus of instruction. Rather, roles and responsibilities are tools that support literacy learning during literature study groups.

Once Tim has established a productive and supportive learning community and has engaged kids in extensive read-aloud conversations, he begins literature study groups. For the first literature study, he chooses a text they will read together as a class, such as *Charlotte's Web* by E. B. White (1952). He reminds them of the strategies that help them interpret texts before, during, and after reading (e.g., picture walk to make predictions before reading, sticky note connections and questions during reading, written conversations after reading). Then they walk through the process together as a class. Since he knows it is impossible for one book to be a perfect match for all readers' interests and/or abilities, Tim selects a book that seems to be the best fit possible. He employs strategies such as partner reading and shared reading during in-class reading time to offer additional support for kids who may need it. He also includes strategies for using the class chapter book as a bedtime story and encourages parents to devise ways to help their young readers at home (Jennings, 2002).

Tim wants children to see literature study as a chance to explore and celebrate great literature. He wants them to interact meaningfully with others enjoying the same book. For some, the first few literature study texts may be easy to read on their own. Others will need considerable support. Children are encouraged to read in pairs or in small groups. Tim also reads lengthy passages aloud with small groups and, at times, to the entire class.

Parents are invited into the literature study as well. Tim suggests in newsletters that parents keep up with the reading and hold conversations about the book with their children at home. Parents often ask how they can help. Through weekly correspondence in newsletters, Tim keeps parents informed of the children's progress in literature study and ways in which parents can support their young readers (see Chapter 5 for examples of newsletters).

Tim also creates a literature response journal for children to use each day. Typically, students use the literature response journal as a way to respond through art and writing to passages in a text before coming together to talk about the book. That way all of the children are poised to share insights, connections, questions, interesting language, and other recorded thoughts. Literature response journals are tools that allow the students and Tim to help foster substantive conversations. A new book is designed, with the students' input, before each new literature study. Tim doesn't treat the written responses as an end in themselves. While responses are required, they are mainly used as a reference in small- and large-group conversations. Often the children use their written reflections as a way to start the book talks (for example, everyone might share a favorite passage from the chapter), and the talk often proceeds from there. The written responses often initiate the conversation, but the conversation quickly moves to new places not recorded on anyone's response sheet. Additionally, literature response frameworks vary from time to time. While some features are consistent over time, they are not static. During a recent literature study in second grade with *Charlotte's Web,* for instance, Tim invited the kids to codesign the literature response form for this particular book. Kelly suggested the class record information about their reading strategies. This was not something Tim had anticipated, but he gladly incorporated the suggestion into the literature response journals he prepared for everyone (see Figures 2.3a and b).

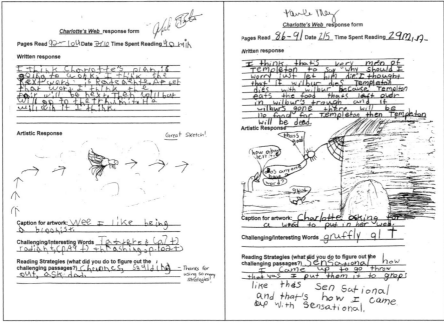

Figure 2.3a/b. Two children's literature response journal entries for *Charlotte's Web*. Figure 2.3a also shows some of Tim's comments on the journal entry.

Tim has found scaffolding literature study groups from whole-class to small-group conversations essential to their success. He wants the kids initially to live the process together with extensive support, and then he gradually releases control (Cambourne, 1988). When Tim initiated literature circles with his current class of second graders, he employed the following strategies, using *Charlotte's Web* as the foundational text:

- Collaborate with the children to design the literature response journal.

- Read the first two chapters together as a shared reading experience.

- Talk about the text together as a whole class and respond to the reading as a class using the literature response journal.

- Gradually release control by asking kids to read about three chapters a week and begin literature responses and conversations in small groups.

- Eventually, the children begin selecting their own texts and response strategies.

- The children make the texts and the processes for responding and conversing their own.

How Literature Circles Look and Sound

Being able to see in practice how Tim and other teachers at the Center use literature as a means of learning through language while contributing to a democratic education is best revealed within the context of an authentic conversation. For that reason, we have included a complete transcript of a conversation that Tim and some of his second graders had about the short story "The Tree House" (Lowry, 1990).

The conversation took place during a focus study on peace and freedom. The children had read "The Tree House" independently or with partners and marked sections they wanted to bring to their literature study conversation. The story is about two neighbors, Chrissy and Leah.

> Chrissy's grandfather had just built Chrissy a terrific tree house. Better than terrific. It was a marvelous, magnificent, one-of-a-kind tree house, with wooden walls painted bright blue. It had two windows with red shutters on each and a yellow door with two shiny brass hinges and a small brass bell that rang when you pulled the string. (Lowry, 1990, p. 30)

Chrissy doesn't want to share her house with anyone, including her neighbor. Even though Chrissy makes a sign that says KEEP OUT, Leigh comes over. Chrissy won't let her in, and Leigh is devastated. Leigh's father is out of work, so he has the time to take old boards from the corner of his yard and build a tree house for his daughter. The second tree house is not as fancy on the surface. Conflict between the two girls escalates until they realize that both tree houses are lovely in their own ways and that it would be much more satisfying to play together than to compare and criticize.

Several groups of Tim's students are holding literature conversations simultaneously, and there is a focused hum in the room. Tim joins a group and functions as a participant and guide. We include the entire transcript here to provide readers a genuine sense of the rhythm, content, and roles of the teacher and kids in such conversations. As a teacher-researcher, Tim often records small-group and whole-class conversations to capture and interpret the nature of talk and learning across the day. On this day, like most, there are moments of brilliance, lots of typical kid talk, as well as times when Tim pushes the conversation forward.

> *Mr. O'Keefe:* [Speaking into the tape recorder] This is Ali, Elaina, and Joe. Ali, what were you saying?
>
> *Ali:* I was reading what I highlighted.

Mr. O'Keefe: Is that how you guys have been doing it, reading what you marked?

Elaina: She was reading what she highlighted, then she . . . she highlighted stuff and then she read a line from it and wrote what she thought of it.

Mr. O'Keefe: Okay, I'm sorry.

Ali: And I highlighted, *Finally she called across the fence. "Would you like to borrow some of mine?" she asked. And Leah said, "Yes."* And Chrissy is finally trying to be nice, I think. At first she was really mean, then she started to be nice. And just about where they made the bridge and I wrote, "I like their idea." Then I highlighted, *"I don't really hate you, Leah," Chrissy said. "I don't really hate you either," Leah replied. They sat together on the porch and looked around happily.* "I'm glad they're getting along," is what I wrote, is what I wrote.

Mr. O'Keefe: Can you say things to each other after you say stuff? You know how Ali highlighted the part about the bridge? In my notes, I wrote that the bridge is a metaphor. It's almost like they were at war, but the bridge . . .

Elaina: . . . connected them.

Mr. O'Keefe: That's a good way to put it. It's like a symbol for them becoming connected again.

Elaina: When they were mad, it's like the bridge was a friend-ship line. When they were mad, they would go across.

Mr. O'Keefe: Are you going to share in this, Joe?

Joseph: I wrote, " I wonder if it was a he or she"; I wrote that before I know that they were both girls. I was wondering about where it said, *You reached it by climbing a ladder, a ladder. . . .*

Mr. O'Keefe: But read the whole sentence.

Joseph: You reached it by climbing a ladder, a ladder to the best tree house ever.

Mr. O'Keefe: Did anyone else notice that it was kind of odd that the author said *a ladder* twice? Joe said to me earlier that it was probably a typo.

Elaina: It's not a typo. It's just like, I'm just using this as an example. "I went up a ladder, a ladder." It's just repeating the same word twice. There's nothing really wrong with it.

Mr. O'Keefe: It's just an effect that the author is trying for?

Joseph: . . . *a ladder; a ladder* . . . It shouldn't have it twice.

Elaina: It's like you're stuttering on a word or something.

Joseph: . . . *a ladder; a ladder* . . .

Mr. O'Keefe: Here's another example: "I had some money, some money for some ice cream." It's just an effect.

Ali: It's like, "His name was Sam, Sam the seahorse."

Mr. O'Keefe: Say it again; listen to this.

Ali: His name was Sam, Sam the seahorse.

Mr. O'Keefe: That's a good connection.

Elaina: But it's not a typo; it's not wrong. . . .

Joseph: . . . *a ladder; a ladder.*

Elaina: It's an effecto! Instead of a grammero, it's an effecto.

Mr. O'Keefe: It's an effecto.

Joseph: It's like saying the same sentence twice.

Mr. O'Keefe: It's like saying the same words twice, isn't it? Is there anything else you wrote besides those kinds of things, or anything else you just think of?

Joseph: I wrote that Chrissy is going to be best friends with Leah again.

Mr. O'Keefe: So, you wrote that before the end of the story?

Joseph: And I got it right.

Mr. O'Keefe: That's right. Good prediction. [Turning to Elaina.] Did you have a chance to share your stuff yet?

Elaina: I noticed that there's an alliteration at the beginning of the book because it says, *marvelous, magnificent, marvelous, magnificent,* and as I said, it was alliteration. Afterwards I thought it was like a very deep thought . . . *two shiny brass hinges and a small brass bell that rang when you pulled the string.*

Mr. O'Keefe: That's a nice description of the tree house. Even if you didn't have a picture, you could kind of imagine it.

Elaina: And it said . . . *It all mine, isn't it?* on page 31 at the very top, close to the very top. I thought it was just . . . kind of bratty, I'm going to say. Then it says . . . *just mine and nobody else?* That's selfish!

Mr. O'Keefe: The way you read that was just the way I heard it in my head.

Elaina: Because they're just diagonal from each other, so maybe the author tried to make it that way. I think why she wrote *Keep Out* and stuff, I think it's sort of . . . their grandfather started this because he's the one who said . . . If he would have said that everybody else could play in it too, she probably would have let everybody else in.

Joseph: But her grandpa said that it was just for her.

Elaina: It's like her grandpa influenced her to say that.

Joseph: It's like Saddam. No, like Hitler. He made the people think that the Jews were bad.

Elaina: He made them believe that the Jews were their trouble.

Joseph: And the guy made Chrissy think that Leah was bad.

Mr. O'Keefe: You know, I didn't look at it that way. I can certainly see exactly what you're saying. The way I looked at it was . . . She said you made this for me, it's all mine, right? He said, "That's right, I made it for you." I don't think he was saying, "You can't have other people here." But he was saying, "That's right, I made it for you, I didn't make it for someone else I don't know."

Ali: She didn't understand probably.

Mr. O'Keefe: I think she understood it the way she wanted to understand it.

Ali: She's probably thinking, well, it's mine. I can do whatever I want with it.

Elaina: She didn't understand the way *he* was telling *her*. And then I wrote, "It's beautiful" on page 31 close to the bottom. Then I wrote "good detail." I underlined *I hate you, Chrissy. I hate you.* I wrote that they were kind of acting . . . in my way I'd say cuckoo.

Mr. O'Keefe: I thought they were getting a little carried away too. It was mean for Chrissy to say, "No."

Elaina: No, the first one to say "I hate you" was Leah because she wouldn't let her in.

Mr. O'Keefe: So Chrissy was mean by saying, "No you can't come in. This is my tree house." Leah got immediately carried away. Instead of just getting her feelings hurt, she just started hurting the other person.

Elaina: [quoting from the story] *She stood silently for a moment. Then she said, "I hate you, Chrissy." Then Chrissy goes, "I hate you too."*

Joseph: If she whispered it, how could Chrissy hear her? They were like in a yard.

Ali: I think that Leah got a little bit carried away. Maybe she shouldn't have said, "I hate you." She might have said, "That's mean. Maybe you shouldn't be so mean," or something like that.

Joseph: Chrissy said, "I hate you too."

Elaina: Joe, it's not really her fault. Chrissy started it.

Mr. O'Keefe: Joe, what you said about whispering, I think she said it in a soft voice, but apparently she said it in a loud enough voice so the other kid could hear.

Joseph: She was up in the tree house. And she was on the ground. That would be counting how high the tree was.

Mr. O'Keefe: Maybe it wasn't actually a whisper. Maybe it was sort of like [speaking in a low voice], "I hate you." It wasn't a scream; I don't know, that's a good point. Maybe *whisper* wasn't the right choice for a word there.

Elaina: I highlighted . . . *He was making Leah a tree house. Chrissy laughed to herself. She knew they didn't have extra money now for things like paint and brass hinges.* And I also did . . . *never in a million years.* I thought just because she has paint and brass hinges it doesn't mean that it's better than somebody else's.

Joseph: Leah's was better than hers.

Elaina: It just means she's got more than she does. Wow.

Joseph: Leah had all those pictures on her wall and she had . . .

Elaina: . . . curtains, fruit . . .

Joseph: . . . wastebasket.

Ali: Chrissy didn't really have that stuff. She said, *"I don't really have curtains or a rug."*

Mr. O'Keefe: They both lied a little bit, didn't they?

Ali: Just to brag. They wanted to be better than the other one.

Elaina: I wrote that doesn't mean anything. Then I went over *Do you have any books I can borrow?* Then she starts to be a little kinder.

Mr. O'Keefe: That was the turning point in the story, wasn't it?

Elaina: Yep! Then they turned around like they were going back to being friends like they were.

Mr. O'Keefe: I like the way you made that little, little swirl, that does kind of . . . that's sort of a symbol for turning around.

Elaina: Then I wrote that they started telling the truth to each other instead of keep lying, and lying and lying, keep making up more lies. And then I thought, Lora was my partner, and when it says that the board would go from your house to my porch, over the top of the fence and they could visit each other by walking across the board, I went hooo, very scary!

Ali: I don't know how a fence could be that low, you know, to get to the porch.

Joseph: It would probably be the tree house porch.

Ali: No, she means the fence is about to your height, then put the whatever-you-call-it on top.

Elaina: I thought she meant from the porches on the house, but maybe she meant from the tree house porches.

Mr. O'Keefe: I think it's the tree house porches; is that what you guys thought too?

Ali: Yes, they put the wooden board—see they were next-door neighbors, and they put the wooden board on the side of the tree house and then it would connect to the other side of the other person's tree house and then they could walk across.

Joseph: But what happened, they would have to be the same length and height.

Mr. O'Keefe: Right, well, they could slant a little. They would have to be pretty much the same height, you're right.

Ali: Right now, I'm on the side of Chrissy, because she says, *Chrissy eyed the distance and the height. "What if we fell?"* It must be pretty wide if they can hold hands, and pretty long.

Mr. O'Keefe: It must be like a plank or something; it doesn't even show the picture of it.

Elaina: Ali, it says right here that a *wide board, wide board.*

Mr. O'Keefe: There were two things that I thought were great metaphors. One was the fence. It's something that divides people, right? Like, this is your property, this is my property. And then the board, or the bridge, is what connects people. So, even though this is not a true story, I mean it could happen, but it is not a true story, I don't think. But I love the way that she used those things and I think she did it real obviously as a metaphor—the fence, the things that divides us.

Elaina: I thought it was kind of cute when it says, *"It's not very high,"* Leah pointed out. *"If we each came out half way and held hands we could help each other across."*

Clearly, these children are learning language. They are doing what good readers do, reading and talking about the text in careful yet passionate ways and asking questions of the text and one another. They are living a reading-as-inquiry model, and they are continuing to learn that reading is a transactive process (Rosenblatt, 1995). They are not necessarily looking for the meaning within the text or the teacher. Instead, they share and negotiate the meaning they are constructing throughout the conversation.

They are learning about language in important ways as well. The children had been spotting typos in professionally published work and sharing their observations in the class language journal during the morning meeting. On this day, they hold a debate about the author's decision to repeat the phrase "a ladder." One child obviously thinks it was an improper decision, while others think it might have been included intentionally for effect. Elaina transforms the conversation by arguing that it isn't a "typo." In fact, it isn't even a "grammero." She names the strategy an "effecto." By doing so in the group, and later with the class, Elaina helps everyone in this class culture think about breaking conventions for effect. They are learning about how they can dance with language by breaking conventions intentionally (Ray, 2002). Additionally, they continue learning about language by exploring the author's use of metaphor, symbolism, and alliteration.

The children are also learning through language before, during, and after the reading. They make intertextual ties with insights that had emerged during morning meeting conversations about current events, specifically about how Saddam Hussein influenced people. They also revisit a topic that Joseph had investigated during his expert project on the Holocaust. While Tim doesn't see the grandfather's influence in precisely the same way as the children do, he acknowledges the connections they make and is pleased that they are probing beneath the surface to critically analyze this text in light of others they have experienced together. Finally, this story and the conversation that ensues give the students a chance to further explore the strengths and struggles involved in friendship and the problems that grow out of useless competition. They learn more about typical issues that elementary children face through this lovely story and provocative conversation. They leave the conversation with new insights about friendship, one another, and the concept of peace they have been exploring together.

Writing Workshop

Writing workshop in Tim's room reflects many of the principles and practices inherent in the authoring cycle model developed by Short and Harste (1996). In fact, the curricular framework for writing workshop is based on central features of the authoring cycle. Tim and his students, however, have made the model their own over the years by looking within and reflecting on what works best as they strive to grow and change as authors. As Fletcher and Portalupi suggest, "We don't want to teach our students *the* writing process; rather, we want each one of them to find *a* process that works for him or her. This process will inevitably differ from student to student" (2001, p. 62). Tim and his students have also looked outside of the classroom to distant teachers, such as favorite picture and chapter book authors like Patricia Polacco, Karen Hesse, Cynthia Rylant, and Sharon Creech, as well as to leaders in the teaching of writing such as Ralph Fletcher, Lucy Calkins, and Katie

Wood Ray, to help them envision possible structures and strategies that will best support each and every author in the classroom.

While Tim honors the unique needs and strengths of each writer, he also recognizes the importance of a flexible yet predictable structure that will hold writing time together and move it forward. Tim and the children have coauthored a predictable structure for writing workshop. Although Tim encourages the children to use particular processes and strategies when publishing, writing workshop is not a formulaic activity.

Getting Started

When Tim gets a new group of second graders from kindergarten-first-grade teacher Jennifer Barnes, he knows he can count on the fact that they have been writing to learn and communicate since they were in kindergarten. He knows he can assume they will be comfortable taking risks as writers. He also knows that the majority of them will love to write and cherish writing workshop time. So he begins the year by helping them learn how to take pieces from their writer's notebooks through the authoring cycle. They focus on the ways in which author's circles and editing conferences can help them learn to think and grow as authors. Tim works hard to help them understand that the authoring cycle is not about going through the motions. Rather, it is about helping kids learn to write for an audience; how to write like readers and read like writers; and how to learn the craft, skills, and strategies that good writers use. It is about learning to use writing to entertain, inform, and move others. It is also about using writing to better understand yourself and the world in which you live and breathe.

Tim begins the year by walking the kids through the process together using an open-ended yet focused topic such as family stories (Short & Harste, 1996). The family story focus provides unity and common literacy experiences, both of which are important at the beginning of the year. It also promotes choice and ownership since there are as many story possibilities as there are children in the class. While the topic works well to initiate the authoring cycle, it also helps build classroom community. The teacher and children learn to care for one another in new ways by delighting in one another's joyful pieces and sharing the sorrow that emerges when they compose stories about pain and loss. At the same time, Tim uses magnificent children's books from a family story text set for class read-alouds.

Tim also demonstrates and then engages the children in different features of the process, such as author's circles and self-editing. Using an authentic family story he is composing, he uses think-alouds to show the kids how these processes work for him as an author. He also invites kids to continually reflect on what they are learning throughout the process, such as how to find a topic, how to make revisions based on feedback from friends, how to help an author, and so forth. Naturally, he posts their insights throughout the room as a reference tool, which helps the children understand why each feature of the process matters.

Once they take their pieces through the authoring cycle, the students hold an author's celebration. The children read their personal family stories to their friends, teacher, and parents in small groups. Each member of the audience responds by sharing what they noticed or liked about the piece. They write their observations on sticky notes and give them to the author to place in the back of the book as a record of the author's accomplishments. Tim also invites parents to read and respond to their young authors using the same format. The children cherish comments from their friends, family, and teacher.

After internalizing ways of living and learning together during writing workshop, the students begin to truly think, work, and publish as authors. Once they get started, kids soon fall into different rhythms as authors. Tim creates timelines and expectations for the group, keeping track of the students' progress but in ways that allow them to work independently while maintaining choice and ownership of their topics. On any given day, some will be drafting prewriting ideas, others will be writing furiously, still others will be holding author's circles with peers or editing conferences with a parent or their teacher. In second and third grade, Tim finds that about four to five children complete and publish pieces during each writing workshop.

Writing Workshop Schedule

Tim and his students follow a predictable schedule to structure their time during writing workshop. While this schedule is necessarily flexible, it is also highly predictable. Kids know they can count on time for uninterrupted writing; time to hold content conferences with their friends, parents, or teacher; time to receive help editing; and time to revise, edit, and publish. The children also know they can count on learning about language during a minilesson and strategy sharing time at the end of workshop.

Typical Workshop Schedule

9:30–9:35	Inspirational poem and settling-in time
9:35–9:45	Quiet writing

9:45–10:30	Workshop (writing, author's circles, editing conferences, etc.)
10:30–10:45	Minilesson and strategy sharing
10:45–11:00	Publishing

Features of Writing Workshop: An Explanation

Inspirational Poem and Settling-in Time

Workshop begins by reciting a poem together. The following poem is one of the children's favorites:

> Only as high as I
>   reach can I grow
> Only as far as I
>   seek can I go
> Only as deep as I
>   look can I see
> Only as much as I
>   dream can I be.
>   –Anonymous

Next, Tim reminds them of the craft lessons, skills, and strategies they have been exploring most recently. Then they gather their writer's notebooks and materials together and settle in for independent writing.

Quiet Writing

Over the past couple of years, Tim has found it invaluable to begin writing workshop with ten to fifteen minutes of quiet, uninterrupted writing. This gives Tim and the children a chance to reread their pieces and immerse themselves in the process without distractions. When given the gift of quiet writing time, the children continue writing in focused ways after finding their rhythm as authors. Tim has also noticed that the rest of workshop is more productive when kids reconnect with their pieces before moving to more social engagements such as author's circles and editing conferences. Because Tim believes it is important to write in front of and alongside the children, he writes during this time as well, allowing him to live the process with his students. It also allows him the time and space he needs to function as a writing coach by conferring with the children on content, craft, and conventions during the workshop time that follows. Tim, however, like all teachers, has students who need additional guidance. It's not that they don't value the chance to be independent; it's that they don't always make good use of their time or function consistently as resourceful authors. So Tim has developed a habit of conducting regular spot-checks around the room between conferences and offering guidance to those who need it. He attempts to create an atmosphere in which children feel his presence whether he is sitting next to them or across the room (Anderson, 2000). The reality is that some children need a physical touch or gentle nudge occasionally to stay focused and productive.

Workshop

During workshop time, Tim and parent volunteers assist the young authors in a number of ways. They help kids talk through their plans when they are "in the midst" of writing. They help children conduct author's circles and make changes based on the feedback they have received. They hold editing conferences with individuals. They talk through their editorial suggestions with the children. Through these activities, they are teaching the kids how language conventions function to support the text and improve communication between author and reader. In short, they hold intimate minilessons on how and why skills and language conventions are used.

During this time, children find comfortable places to work and immerse themselves in the process of creating and refining texts. Sometimes they access a peer sitting near them for support; other times they request a conference with an adult. In general, the children learn to be resourceful during workshop. They know who to ask for help with spelling; who might be able to give them the best advice on an effective transition; who might help them think of synonyms for words they overuse; who might help them illustrate their final draft; and so on. They know it is their responsibility to write intensively and extensively as well as help others in need during this time (see Figure 2.4).

Once children have taken their pieces through the authoring cycle and have had successful adult editing conferences, they are invited to publish their writing. Some children publish by transferring their final draft into a bound book complete with illustrations. Others simply write the final draft on a clean, crisp piece of paper. The children select the final format based on the content and form of the piece. Some children who become especially inspired by poetry collections create poetry books and add to them regularly. Basically, the children know they are ready to go public with their work once they have attended to their audience and have taken the time and care necessary to put their writing into final form.

Figure 2.4. Tim and students engaged in writing workshop activities.

Minilesson and Strategy Sharing

Tim plays cleanup music to signal the end of workshop. The kids put their materials away and come to the carpet for a writing minilesson and strategy sharing time. They know to bring their notebooks to the class meeting if Tim is going to feature their work.

Tim opens the minilesson by making connections between the craft, skill, or strategy the students have been exploring together as authors and what he wants to introduce or revisit. He always contextualizes his minilessons by sharing what he has noticed kids doing as authors, questions they have posed, or insights they have constructed when discussing qualities of good literature during read-alouds or literature study. Next he takes a few minutes to show the group a skill (language conventions such as spelling, grammar, or punctuation) and/or craft (writing leads, describing the setting, character development, circle stories, using language patterns for effect, word choice, voice, etc.).

Tim looks for patterns in his kidwatching notes and written artifacts to decide which skill or craft to highlight on a particular day. He considers the standards he is expected to teach at each grade level and reveals them at the time he thinks they will be most helpful to his young authors. Most important, he makes instructional decisions based on his students' strengths, needs, and interests. While he foregrounds the state standards during minilessons, Tim certainly doesn't limit the lessons to them. He relies on his own experiences as a writer and on his writer's notebook to create curriculum (Ray, 2002). He also relies on the expertise of distant teachers such as Ralph Fletcher, Donald Graves, Lucy Calkins, and Carl Anderson. Their advice extends the content of the state standards and provides substantive writing strategy and craft lessons. In other words, he teaches the standards and so much more.

Although Tim plans what he wants to address before workshop begins and has drafted a demonstration lesson, he also looks for instances of the skill or craft in use during workshop time. Then he highlights the skill or craft by using the children's work and his own to show what it looks like in use. Often, he invites the children to share their work and explain the process they used to the class, thus validating the kids as authors and illuminating how they can learn from one another. This ritual also encourages children to reflect on their own work and explain how, when, and why they use particular skills or strategies. The more the children reflect on and explain their thinking, the greater control they gain over the process.

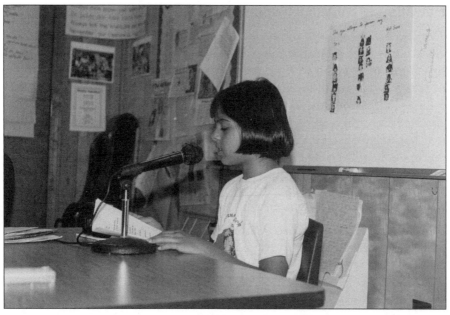

Figure 2.5. A student publishing her work at the close of writing workshop.

Publishing

The class concludes each writing workshop with publishing. The children look forward to hearing and responding to their friends' publications as much as they enjoy sitting in the author's chair. We have learned that many children push themselves to grow as writers because of the valuable feedback they receive from their teacher and peers during "celebrating authorship."

Once the children have completed a published piece, they put it in the publishing pile. Tim makes space in the schedule for about four to five children to publish every Tuesday and Thursday. The children read their pieces into a microphone, making it easier to hear and appreciate the language used (see Figure 2.5). The microphone elevates the significance of the event and makes it possible for all voices to be heard. After reading their publications and sharing corresponding illustrations, the authors call on their friends and teacher to give them feedback. The audience responds with comments and questions. The comments often consist of compliments about the content and form of the piece, and questions often reflect genuine inquiry, such as: Where did you get your idea for that story? Are you going to make a sequel? After the author calls on several members of the audience to respond, the class applauds and the next young author settles into the author's chair.

How Writing Workshop Looks and Sounds

Tim and his colleagues at the Center welcome so many visitors into their classrooms each year that the children in Tim's class decided to create a brochure to describe writing workshop. When visitors enter the room or when a parent volunteers, the kids distribute the brochure to explain what is happening and how parents and visitors might join in. The brochure represents writing workshop through the children's eyes (see Figure 2.6). They designed it and took it through the authoring cycle before going public with it. Their explanation of each phase of the process demonstrates their understanding and appreciation of the authoring cycle.

Minilessons and Strategy Sharing

In Chapter 3, Tim describes the importance of teaching each writer and includes excerpts from writing conferences with two very different children. So here we focus on whole-group minilessons and strategy sharing.

Minilesson

Tim noticed that the time was right to focus on setting; he knew he needed to focus his students' attention on setting to help them grow as writers. At the same time, he wanted to do some work with poetry. And so he brought both together through craft lessons and haiku. He introduced haiku to the group by first reading from a book of poetry. Together they analyzed the Japanese nature poetry by discussing what they noticed about the structure. Then Tim summarized and clarified their observations by pointing out that all the poems focus on nature and all consist of three lines. The first line has five syllables, the second line has seven syllables, and the third line has five syllables. Next they created some haiku together as a class, with Tim writing their ideas on the board as the students generated them. He paused while they counted syllables for each line. Tim referred to syllables as "chunks of sound within words." He reminded the children that all haiku is about nature and uses the outdoors as the setting. As usual, he challenged them to try out a new form of writing during writing workshop. This was an invitation, not an assignment, and the children knew it. Some seized the chance immediately and others waited and watched their friends try their hand at haiku before delving in themselves.

Strategy Sharing

After writing workshop, Tim invited the kids who had composed haiku or pieces about the setting in their current writing to share. Although

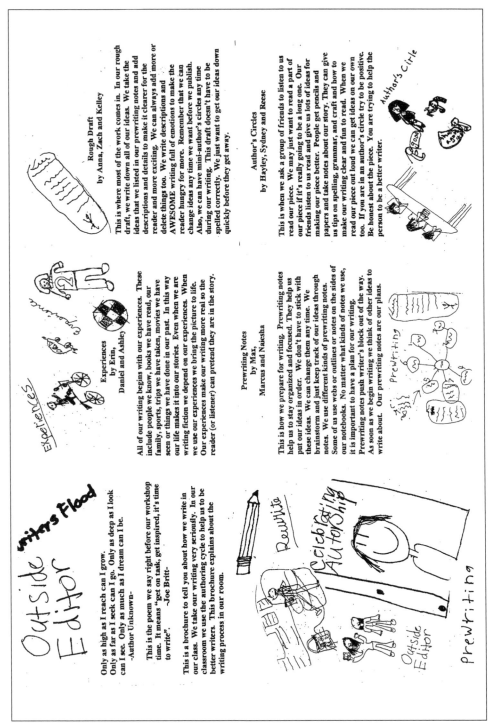

Outside Editor

Only as high as I reach can I grow.
Only as far as I seek can I go. Only as deep as I look
can I see. Only as much as I dream can I be.
–Author Unknown–

This is the poem we say right before our workshop
time. It means "get on task, get inspired, it's time
to write".

This is a brochure to tell you about how we write in
our class. We take our writing very seriously. In our
classroom we use the authoring cycle to help us to be
better writers. This brochure explains about the
writing process in our room.

Experiences
by Erin,
Daniel and Ashley

All of our writing begins with our experiences. These
include people we know, books we have read, our
family, sports, trips we have taken, movies we have
seen or things we have done in our past. In this way
our life makes it into our stories. Even when we are
writing fiction we depend on our experiences. When
we use our experiences we bring the picture to life.
Our experiences make our writing more real so the
reader (or listener) can pretend they are in the story.

Prewriting Notes
by Max,
Marcus and Naiesha

This is how we prepare for writing. Prewriting notes
help us to stay organized and focused. They help us
put our ideas in order. We don't have to stick with
these ideas. We can change them any time. We
brainstorm and just keep track of our ideas through
notes. We use different kinds of prewriting notes.
Some of us use webs or outlines or notes on the sides of
our notebooks. No matter what kinds of notes we use,
it is important to have a plan for our writing.
Prewriting notes push writer's block out of the way.
As soon as we begin writing we think of other ideas to
write about. Our prewriting notes are our plans.

Rough Draft
by Anna, Zach and Kelley

This is where most of the work comes in. In our rough
draft, we write down all of our ideas. We take the
ideas that we listed in our prewriting notes and add
descriptions and details to make it clearer for the
reader and more exciting. We can always add more or
delete things too. We write descriptions and
AWESOME writing full of emotions to make the
reader hungry for more. Remember that we can
change ideas any time we want before we publish.
Also, we can have mini-author's circles any time
during our writing. This draft doesn't have to be
spelled correctly. We just want to get our ideas down
quickly before they get away.

Author's Circles
by Hayley, Sydney and Reese

This is when we ask a group of friends to listen to us
read our piece. We may just want to read a part of
our piece if it's really going to be a long one. Our
friends listen to us read and give us lots of ideas for
making our piece better. People get pencils and
papers and take notes about our story. They can give
us tips on spelling, grammar, and craft and how to
make our writing clear and fun to read. When we
read our piece out loud we can get ideas on our own
too. If you are in an author's circle try to be positive.
Be honest about the piece. You are trying to help the
person to be a better writer.

Figure 2.6. The students' brochure describing writing workshop to classroom visitors.

Figure 2.6 continued

Revisions and Self-Editing
by Erika, Austin and Melanie

After we've had an author's circle, our friends have just given us ideas about how to make our piece better. In revisions we add good ideas from our author's circle to our story. We do not *have* to make the changes they suggested but if they are good suggestions they will only make our story better. We also go back through our piece and try to fix as many of the writing mechanics as possible (capitalization, spelling, punctuations). We may want to circle some of our words if we are not sure how they are spelled. This will help the editor to know what we need to work on. Dictionaries will help us to spell better too.

Outside Editor/Rewrite
by Kristen, Lydia and Will

When we have finished with our revisions we take our piece to an outside editor. These are often parents, visitors, an MAT or the teacher. They will help us to fix our work. They are sort of like an extra author's circle. They will also help us with spelling, punctuation and capital letters. They may give us advice about our handwriting. When we work with an outside editor *we really have to work together*. We don't just give it to them and expect them to edit it for us. We pay attention because we can learn more about writing because we can see what we've missed and learn from it and remember it next time. When we are done working with the editor we rewrite our piece the very best we can. We should try to write neatly and get all of the CHPS right (capitals, handwriting, punctuation, and spelling). We write our final draft on clean paper or in a blank book. We may want to put a cover on it and decorate the cover. When we finish we are ready to publish.

Publishing/Celebrating Authorship
by Joe, David, Kaila

This is the last part of the authoring cycle. This is when we sit in the big chair (the publishing chair) and read our stories to the class. We read into the microphone so others can hear us easily. When we are done sharing them the class applauds. We are glad we have done it. The class raises hands to make positive comments and to ask questions. Then we take our pieces home and read them to our parents. They make comments on sticky notes and we take them back to class. Then we read the comments out loud to the class. Then we put them in our files or the book rack so the other kids can read them again if they want to.

Writer's Block
by Will, Erin and Joe

This is simply when you block. You can't think of anything to write about. This is the opposite of *Writer's Flood*. You just run out of ideas. It is kind of like a dam. You know there are ideas there but they won't come out. You feel like your brain is frozen. Here are some ideas to help with writer's block: sit in some author's circles, read something great, do some free writing – just write about anything until you come across a new idea, go back to something you have written before and make it even better. Just whining about it won't help. It may even make it worse.

Writer's Flood
By Kelley, Joe,
Courtney and Will

This is the opposite of *Writer's Block*. This is when you are really inspired. You have a sea of ideas all flowing through your mind. It's like when a river gets too much rain. Your pencil just can't keep up with your brain. You should take advantage of this! Jot down ideas as fast as you can. One thing you can do is go to the back of your notebook and write down every idea that comes into your head. When you are back to normal you will have a great long list of things to write about in the future. These can be combined sometimes to make really creative writing.

all of the children have a chance to publish a variety of pieces and share their work regularly, this ritual encourages the kids to try out the strategy, skill, or craft featured in a minilesson and to share it with their classmates. Sharing work in progress as well as final drafts inspires kids to push themselves as writers. Tim has created a culture of writers, a group of kids who treasure the chance to share their writing and thinking about writing. They often take turns "speaking into the silence" (DuVall, 2001) by simply reading their pieces and reveling in the beauty and power of the language.

Tim: If you have a haiku you have to read, please share it.

Naiesha: Winter is awesome
It is very, very cold
I love the winter.

Erin: The sweet smell of nature
When leaves fall
It glitters the forest.

Reece: Flowers are awesome
They smell sweet and look pretty
Flowers are awesome

Will: They noticed it was quite beautiful
With the weeping willows close to the river
And the river running so fastly

Tim: That is pretty. I bet you were describing your setting, weren't you? Did you count the syllables?

Will: Well, I put it in my story.

Tim: That's a nice way to incorporate it; you can put poetry inside your story.

Miss Adams (USC intern/student teacher): Butterflies flutter
Their delicate wings aglow
Their antenna poised

Tim: Nice images.

Diane Bonneville (parent): I float softly down
Momentary perfection
Suspended in silk

Can anyone guess what this is about?

Will: The things that go over the windows.

Zach: A spider?

Tim: Listen to it again.

Diane: I float softly down
Momentary perfection
Suspended in silk

Zach: Like a spider coming down.

Tim: What do you think, Kayla?

Kayla: Spider's web? A silkworm?

Will: Is it the bug or whatever inside the silk?

Diane: I noticed when it snowed last week that the snowflakes would fall directly on the spiderweb; you could see all of the facets of the snowflake. It was perfect and then it would melt. It was just beautiful. That's what I was trying to capture. Unless you knew that, you wouldn't know what it was about.

Naiesha: Did you take a picture or draw a picture of it?

Diane: No, I didn't.

Tim: She wrote a poem, so now we all have an image of it in our minds.

Zach: Warm and windy day
Waves are crashing on the shore
Cool purple seashells

Tim: You know what is really nice about this is there are all different times of year mentioned in the poems, in the haikus. From warm and windy summertime on the beach to cold and crispy days. So when we are on our walk tomorrow, we are going down to Hidden Pond, you may want to write some haikus to capture that moment for you. Will, I love the fact that you incorporated a haiku right inside your story. I don't know that I have ever noticed anyone doing that before. [Turning to Kelly] Kelly?

Kelly: Well, I like haikus but it is kind of hard to write them because you have to write them in that pattern, 5-7-5.

Tim: That's true. You certainly can write great nature poetry without writing haikus. So if they don't match the syllables, just call it a nice nature poem.

Diane: I noticed that some children thought you had to have one word with five syllables.

Tim: And some kids were counting words and they weren't counting syllables. So it takes some practice. What I found [is] that during quiet writing time I wrote several haikus and then I wanted to go back and just write on my story, and I realized as I was writing my story that I was counting syllables. So it is a different kind of writing, isn't it? It took me a while before I just got back into the storytelling way of writing.

Tim: [Turning back to Kelly] I use my fingers and tap my fingers on the table. You are right. When you are writing haikus, you have to write a little more carefully. Which I think is probably a good exercise sometimes. You have to think so carefully about each word that you write. Each word has to be really important if you are only going to get seventeen syllables in your poem. We'll try it again. I bet people who write haikus often aren't as slow as we are, but I love these images. Oftentimes in books of poetry, you see haikus with a drawing next to it. So if we saw a drawing of a snowflake suspended in silk, we would know exactly what you [looking to Diane] were talking about. Another thing is you want to give your haikus a title. Usually, they have a one-word title. And that would be another way to let us know exactly what you are writing about. But I kind of like the mystery of yours. It was really pretty. [Changing focus] OK, there were a couple of kids who had things they wanted to share involving their settings. If you have something to share from what you wrote today that describes your setting nicely, let's share that now.

Kayla: [Reading her piece aloud] "Let's go to hog forest. When they got to hog forest, they said, it sure is smelly in here. Cold, scary and there were even icicles hanging down from the trees." That was really scary.

Tim: I have a nice image of that one, Kayla.

Nancy: I have a couple of sentences to share. [Reading her piece aloud] "Winter is here, snow is falling. Winter is calling the cold. The strong winds are beating against the house. It snows then rains and storms and then it rains again."

Tim: That's a really nice description of her setting. And another note I wrote to myself when I was reading Nancy Blythe's story is this sounded so much like a Chris Van Allsburg story. I only read about a half-page of it but when you hear the whole thing, I think you are going to notice that too. I have been noticing that so many authors we have been studying have influenced the way you are writing. That's really great. [Turning to another student] Haley had one. You are influenced by an author in your story too, right? Tell the kids about how you ended your story. She does a Harry Potter story, but it is really more influenced by someone else.

Haley: [Reading her piece aloud] "'Harry Potter I've got a surprise for you!' And with that, he ran off into the distance."

Tim: So tell the kids what you told me about the author who influenced you.

Haley: Mary Pope Osborne sort of led me to that ending because she always leaves me hanging to hear more.

Tim: I wrote something in my writer's notebook today. I'm in the middle of a story. It's a true story about what it was like going to a Catholic school when I was a little boy. I described church a little bit because I went to church every day in school. This is the one with the teacher as the antagonist. It says, "The candles by the altar twinkled brightly and air always had the faint smell of smoke and incense." So I included a little bit of visual and a little bit of smell. It doesn't make that much sense by itself but in the context of the whole story it works. [Shifting focus] Lydia has something she is going to share too.

Lydia: [Reading from her notes] "Don't laugh at me. Don't call me names. Don't push, kick or punch."

Tim: Okay, why did you choose that part to share with us now?

Lydia: Because I hear in movies, or I see people kicking or punching in movies, and I just felt like sharing that to the whole class.

Tim: OK, we have several things to be published. Why don't you put your notebooks up and come on back and we'll publish a few things.

With that announcement, the children settled in for celebrating authorship, otherwise known as publishing. After listening to each piece and responding to each author, they washed their hands and went to lunch and recess.

This strategy sharing session demonstrates the rich opportunities the children have to learn about language during this component of writing workshop. They learned more about writing haiku and the syllables involved and strategies for counting syllables; they explored the relationship between art and poetry and about weaving poetry into a narrative text; they learned more about writing settings; and they revisited the importance of creating images as a writer, about using the senses to create poetic texts, and about intentionally studying an author and being inspired to create new kinds of texts. The children were learning language and learning about language through reflection, conversation, and engagement in the process. They were also demonstrating the state standards for writing by:

- applying a process approach to writing
- writing for a variety of purposes
- responding to texts written by others
- creating legible texts

CHAPTER BOOK READ-ALOUD: 12:00–12:15

While the children enjoy recess and love the time they spend laughing and playing with their friends and teacher, they also look forward to their daily chapter book read-aloud. Tim selects class read-alouds in several ways. Sometimes he selects books written by a particular author the class has been studying. Other times he chooses books that connect to or reflect a concept or theme in the curriculum at large. Still other times he chooses a book that is simply a good read or community builder. Regardless, he makes selections carefully and shares his reasoning with the class.

Chapter books are often used as an anchor as well as a springboard in the curriculum. At times, Tim accesses conversations that follow a read-aloud to introduce a new experience or engagement. Recently, for instance, to initiate a serious craft study of setting, Tim highlighted the way Avi describes the setting in *Poppy* (1995) by taking the class to a local pond, where they found a spot and described the setting in their writer's notebooks. They used insights they had reached by studying Avi's strategies to create their own settings during this shared writing experience.

During read-alouds, the class meets together on the carpet and Tim lights the special reading candle to signify the importance of the event. Once the children show him they are ready, he begins reading.

MATH WORKSHOP: 12:15–1:15

General Principles and Practices

Math workshop in Tim's room reflects the same principles set forth by Michael Halliday (1975) for language learning. Tim and Heidi had the privilege of working closely with David Whitin for over five years. During that time, they took the theoretical framework that had guided their work in literacy and transferred it to mathematics because David helped them realize that math is a language too (Whitin & Whitin, 2000). Halliday's work pushed Tim and his collaborators to use a curricular framework that encourages children to learn mathematics, learn about mathematics, and learn through mathematics. David, Heidi, and Tim put it this way:

> Children grow in mathematical literacy when they have regular opportunities to investigate the purposes, processes, and content of the mathematical system. All three aspects are inherent in a

single mathematical experience. The children, as active construc-
tors of their own knowledge, decide which aspect to draw out
for special attention. Their decisions reflect their individual interests and previous experiences as well as their current intentions and interactions with those around them. In addition, teachers sometimes create experiences that highlight one of these
aspects so that the children will attend to it as part of a natural
context. For example, children learn about the various purposes
of mathematics as they measure dinosaur lengths on the playground, interpret results of a personal survey, or calculate the
most economical plan for a field trip.

Learning about mathematics involves learners exploring the
mathematical system itself. Children are encouraged to experiment with how the system works, such as devising their own
recording system to convey their numerical observations. . . . In
written language development, the form of the message develops through use; this is also true in mathematics. Mathematical
literacy is defined not as mere familiarity with numerical symbols but rather as an understanding of the ideas and processes
that the symbols represent. It is this notion that is at the heart of
learning about mathematics.

Learning through mathematics implies that children use mathematics in all subject areas. Mathematics is an integral part of
social studies as children construct maps of their neighborhoods;
it is a useful tool in science investigations as learners keep a daily
tally of the number of eggs laid by the class turtle; and it is a
natural part of the cooking area when the bakers must figure out
how to divide the cookies equally. Mathematical literacy develops in response to personal and social needs. (Whitin, Mills, &
O'Keefe, 1990, p. 11–12)

Although Tim encourages the children to look at the world mathematically, he knows that for them to learn about mathematics, to use
math as a tool for learning through and about the world, to adopt an
inquiry stance toward mathematics, and to practice the skills and strategies involved in it, he needs to provide structured support. So math
workshop is built into the daily life of the classroom. Just like other
teachers in his district, Tim is required to teach particular math concepts
based on the state standards. As a teacher at the Center for Inquiry, he
is provided with the same math texts as other teachers in his district.
But he doesn't simply follow the book. Instead, Tim follows the explorations of his learners, his mathematicians, and uses the official resources
to help support them. In other words, Tim uses the instructional materials as "documents of inspiration rather than prescription" (Pierce,
1999). This means he teaches math in the same way he teaches reading
and writing: by teaching skills and strategies based on his assessment
of his students' strengths, needs, and interests. He teaches the concepts

and strategies during whole-class minilessons and then provides time for the children to try them out—to pose and solve mathematical problems during workshop. He also creates space in which children can reflect on and share strategies. Tim knows he needs to make the mathematical investigations as authentic as possible, and at the same time he knows he needs to provide time for the children to practice concepts and operations needed to solve real problems. During math workshop, the children do work on mathematical exercises, although they spend far less time on these than you would find the typical third-grade classroom spending. Tim strives to have his students practice skills and strategies through application as much as possible. He realizes that the questions he asks and the invitations he provides will influence whether his students develop a functional or a dysfunctional capacity to develop mathematical literacy.

How Math Workshop Looks and Sounds

The children had been discussing their favorite books and authors for some time. The annual school book fair was quickly approaching, so the conversations took on an urgent tone. To help their friends make good choices at the book fair, Susanne Pender, Tim's looping partner at the Center, and her students had recently constructed an extensive catalog with book reviews by the children and distributed it throughout the school. This in turn inspired Tim's students to conduct class surveys and create graphs about books and authors.

Tim followed the children's lead and used their interest in books to focus on gathering, interpreting, and sharing mathematical data. He had noticed their acute interest in books and authors, he told them, so the class would use math workshop to investigate various strategies they could use to better understand and convey their choices. Tim then used several surveys and graphs from *USA Today* to introduce the lesson. He demonstrated the relationship between the questions that guided the construction of their surveys and the answers they found. Tim also led the students in a focused discussion about how each graph conveyed the information in a unique way. Once he felt they had an understanding of the math concepts that underpin graph and survey construction—a state math standard—he invited them to compose questions and then collect, interpret, and display their findings in small groups.

Tim devoted several math workshop periods to this investigation. While engaging in the process was important in and of itself, the questions Tim asked and the way he responded to the kids throughout the process made a significant difference. He asked questions such as:

- Who would like to know this information?
- Where else might we use this survey?
- Now that you've learned this, what are you wondering now?
- What was your question? Do your data help you answer your question?
- How did you gather your information?
- What format did you use and why?
- What have you learned so far?
- Were there any surprises in your data?
- How would the results change if you eliminated one of the choices?
- What caused a struggle? Were you happy with the solution you created?
- Help me understand what you meant.

These questions guided the construction of individual graphs as well as a whole-group reflection on the graphs and surveys. By adopting an inquiry stance, Tim helped the children recognize how math is used as a tool for learning and how it is used to convey information in powerful yet succinct ways. They learned that lots of folks outside the classroom might be interested in their data. Librarians could use it to order books, bookstores could use it to display and promote particular books, parents could use it to make good choices when placing book fair orders, publishers could use it to make wise choices when offering contracts to authors, and so forth. The children not only learned *about* mathematics, but they also learned the math standard and much more. They learned why the standard mattered to begin with. Most important, they learned how being mathematically literate might empower them, how they could use mathematics to make their choices known in the world. They also learned how people might use mathematics to persuade others. In other words, they were learning to use mathematical literacy and language for critique.

FOCUSED STUDIES: 1:15–2:30

General Principles and Practices

Like many teachers at the Center, Tim uses a focused study framework to construct curriculum in the physical and social sciences. We have found that organizing curriculum around broad concepts such as cycles, systems, and change unites learners and the curriculum. Here we show the relationship between the unit of study and the daily life of the classroom. And to further our purposes in this book as a whole, we share the central roles of oral and written language in this curricular structure. We also attempt to illuminate the interconnected nature of the curriculum and show how reading and writing experiences across curricular structures promote growth within units of study. We recommend *Learning Together through Inquiry* (Short et al., 1996) and *From the Ground Up* (Mills & Donnelly, 2001) for in-depth discussions of the development and implementation of focused studies, an exploration beyond the scope of this book.

Tim devotes a significant amount of time each afternoon to focused study work. He is careful to address required topics in the state science and social studies standards, although he rarely approaches them in isolation. Instead, he creates units of study that fall under the umbrella of a broad concept, thereby making natural transitions within and between units of study and across curriculum areas in general. Early in the year of second grade, for instance, Tim might begin with a unit of study on animals and address it conceptually through the lens of growth and change. This allows him to weave in the role of cycles in the change process by helping the children grow tadpoles and hatch moths and butterflies. The concepts of change and cycles then become curricular touchstones across the two years that Tim and his students will live and learn together. This concept will help them better understand weather, the seasons, astronomy, electricity, the body, historical events, plants, and other topics.

While Tim builds curriculum from a solid conceptual framework, he also weaves oral and written language into units of study as much as possible. It is not unusual for children to choose to read nonfiction materials connected to a unit of study during independent reading time. Likewise, it is common to find children writing stories and poems about the topic of a current or recent focused study unit. Children don't naturally isolate disciplines from one another, and we help them understand the holistic nature of knowledge when the disciplinary lines are blurred through inquiry. At the Center for Inquiry, the focus is on teaching readers, writers, mathematicians, scientists, and historians. The children learn to think and communicate as readers, writers, mathematicians, scientists, and historians while also using reading, writing, and math as tools for learning.

How Focused Study Looks and Sounds

Tim was reading *Poppy,* one of his favorite chapter books by one of his favorite authors. He and his young authors found inspiration to create some craft lessons from the eloquent ways in which Avi described the setting. Suddenly, setting mattered in the children's pieces. It mattered because they had discovered the powerful ways it enhanced Avi's story. Tim and his students were reading like writers.

Tim sought out connections for himself and the kids. In the midst of reading *Poppy*, he realized the time was right to engage in owl pellet investigations. (As predators, owls regurgitate the unused remains of their prey. Owl pellets are the undigested teeth, bones, fur, etc., of their food.) The kids were psyched. The investigation would be a natural extension of reading *Poppy*, one that would enrich their understanding of the text as well as their appreciation of natural cycles in the food web. (The connection to *Poppy* is that Poppy's boyfriend, Ragweed, is killed and eaten by Mr. Ocax, the owl, while the two mice are out dancing in the moonlight. Later, when Poppy and her father go to ask Ocax's permission to relocate their family, Poppy discovers Ragweed's earring in an owl pellet under Ocax's tree.)

And so the children set to work, uncovering the artifacts hidden within each pellet. As they investigated, they accessed *Poppy* and nonfiction resources and charts to make sense of their data. As Tim traveled from table to table while children were in the midst of their investigations, he posed questions such as:

- What have you been learning from this project?
- Does the opportunity to investigate owl pellets help you think differently?
- Have you changed your thinking at all about animals and their relationships to other creatures in their surroundings?
- So this food web chart has made a difference to you?
- What were your connections to Poppy?

After extensive collaboration in small groups, Tim invited the class to come together to reflect on connections between *Poppy* and the owl pellet investigation. He didn't want to force the connections but instead let them emerge though both natural table talk and then the formal class reflection session.

> *Tim:* Did you make any connections between *Poppy* and your owl pellets? For me, I read *Poppy* a couple of years ago, but now after doing these owl pellets, I'm thinking differently about the book. It's so much more real to me. I've always known that owls eat mice, but it is so much more realistic to put your fingers on the bones of animals the owl has eaten. What are you writing that you are learning?

Will: I learned that they can see really well.

Tim: What about this experience makes you think that?

Will: *Poppy* helped us see that owls have keen sight and hearing.

Tim: [noticing an unusual silence and so posing the question] Is there anything you learned from doing this that helped you learn more about the book, or anything about the book that helped you learn more about what we are doing now? I think someone did a project on owls earlier in the year. I learned from her that owl's faces are shaped like that so they can collect sound. They are almost like a satellite dish.

Will: I learned that some owls have heart-shaped heads and I learned that porcupines needed salt for their liver in the book of *Poppy.*

Tim: Okay, making a connection to *Poppy.*

Haley: I learned that for real that some people put fake owls on their barns to scare other owls away from eating some of the animals that are in the barn.

Tim: Who else? Back to Zach.

Zach: I didn't know owls ate birds.

Tim: There was a group at table 3 that had bird bones in it, we think. Kayla, you had your hand up.

Kayla: I learned that owls eat a lot and that they eat rodents, shrews, mouses, mole, and voles. And [pointing to her paper] there is a mouse bone.

Erin: I learned that when owls flap their wings they don't make sounds. And how they eat voles, songbirds, insects, and, um, I always thought when we were reading *Poppy* I imagined the owl pellets that it would be small and look like a marble until when I saw it.

Austin: One connection to *Poppy* is that whenever you saw a picture of Poppy after she ran for a long time, you could see her rib bones sticking out. A lot of peoples' bones do that, and if you suck in you would also stick out.

Tim: So you guys found a lot of rib bones in your owl pellet, didn't you?

Austin: And owls eat weasels, shrews, rats, house mouses, deer mice, voles, and some birds. That's a lot of different types of rats and stuff.

Tim: Okay. If you now know something different about the book or if the book made you think differently about this experience with the pellets, please share.

Ashley: I thought when Poppy was there and was fighting the owl I thought she was very brave.

Will: Well, on one of the pictures of Mr. Ocax, I could sort of draw owls better now.

Tim: Okay, seeing that and also maybe hearing the descriptions in the book too helped you as an artist.

Haley: I learned from *Poppy* that Mr. Ocax doesn't just eat mice. I used to think that, but then I found out they eat all kinds of birds and prey.

Kayla: I learned from *Poppy* that they put fake owls up on the barn to keep owls away from the barn to keep the animals safe from the owls who want to get them.

Tim: Thanks. You know, I didn't get a chance to write because I was mostly going around facilitating the groups, but one of the connections that I made between the owl pellet observations and *Poppy* is this: I always knew that owls ate mice and that they produced these little owl pellets and stuff, but seeing one and opening it up and pulling those bones out and cleaning the skulls off, that made me think differently about the predator-prey relationship. I realized that it was there, but when I actually had my hands in those things and I was watching you guys do it, I don't know, I thought about it more seriously. It seemed so much more real. And also, we were reading the tail end of *Poppy* when we were doing the owl pellets, I thought about Mr. Ocax differently. When he ate Ragweed, what he produced was what was left of Ragweed. Not his spirit but just his bones and fur and stuff.

Kids chime in: And his earring.

Tim: Yeah, his earring, right. *Poppy* seemed more real to me when we were doing these owl pellets.

Courtney: Well, just by looking at the front cover of Mr. Ocax, I have learned how to draw owls.

Tim: A couple of kids have mentioned how they are drawing owls in their notebooks.

Tim promoted the skillfulness of inquiry throughout this engagement and reflective conversation. He helped the children develop strategies for learning from primary sources (owl pellets) as well as from distant teachers (Avi). He helped them develop strategies for making sense of their data and making connections across experiences. They were learning through language.

Reflecting on Focus Studies

In general, Tim scaffolds the students' learning during focus studies in the same ways he does when teaching them to read and write. He pays careful attention to what and how they know and then weaves information into the conversation at the time it will connect most. Additionally, he plans experiences carefully to ensure that new connections will be made.

REFLECTION, FRIENDSHIP CIRCLE, AND HOMEWORK: 2:30–2:50

Tim and his students end the day by writing down their homework and gathering their coats and book bags and meeting together on the carpet for one more whole-group session. They reflect on their day, celebrate their accomplishments, and are reminded of any problems or issues that arose and the plans they devised to prevent them from happening again. Tim reminds them of announcements or special newsletter items they need to remember to share with their parents. And with that, they bid one another farewell. Tim gives them each a hug as they cross the threshold out of their classroom.

OFFERING STUDENTS ADDITIONAL SUPPORT THROUGH AFTER-SCHOOL LITERACY CLUB

General Principles and Practices

At the beginning of November, Tim and his students were completing a class literature study of *The Music of Dolphins* by Karen Hesse (1996). This complex text is written in a simple, elegant style, a style that only accomplished authors like Karen Hesse can achieve. Briefly, the story begins off an island near Cuba, where a girl is "rescued" from the ocean by a helicopter. It turns out she had been living with dolphins for years. The girl becomes the subject of serious research on language and learning in the United States. Although at first she thrives, soon she begins to miss her life at sea and starts to regress. In her words, "I must get back to the sea."

Tim describes the experience of studying this book as being especially memorable because he had the chance to share one of his favorite books with some of his best friends. Although most of the children in his class could read the book independently, Tim offered additional literacy support every Wednesday afternoon after school to four of the children. He had invited them to join his Literacy Club at the beginning of the year. Every Wednesday afternoon they shared snacks and stories and engaged in rich literacy experiences together. Tim did not use this time to teach these children differently—just more intently and intimately. As Dick Allington (2001) suggests, struggling readers need

- to read a great deal to become proficient readers
- to have access to appropriate books
- to develop fluency through focused and thoughtful instruction

Tim used this special time of the week to provide additional support in ways that maintained the integrity of the curriculum yet served as a passport to success during daily reading and writing workshops. When the class was in the midst of reading *The Music of Dolphins*, Tim took advantage of Literacy Club time to read and discuss it carefully with these four children. He and his four club members completed literature response forms together, discussed and interpreted the text, and helped one another develop and use effective strategies when they encountered difficult passages. Tim found that the structure of this book enhanced the kids' ability to read it proficiently as well. The middle was quite a challenge for some, but the structure of the beginning and the shared understanding that took place through conversations helped the children interpret the story in stunning ways. The following conversation took place during a Literacy Club meeting.

How After-School Literacy Club Looks and Sounds

Talking about The Music of Dolphins

"I think she is getting back to getting used to eating live fish instead of dead fish," Marcus commented, demonstrating his comprehension of the text.

Chris moved to an interpretation of the text. He remarked, "This is kind of like fighting, fighting for freedom. In this case, um, Mila didn't fight for freedom. She begged for it. Instead, Justin could see that. But it's like Dr. Beck couldn't see anything."

Tim replied, "But her son could see. Dr. Beck, who had this high degree and studied all of these things about human nature and how people think. In some ways, she wasn't as aware as her son."

"It's like she isn't as smart as him," Chris added.

"There is a difference between smartness as far as how much information someone has and common sense. Justin had common sense, didn't he? What were you going to say? I cut you off."

Marcus proceeded, "Mila wants to go back to the sea and Dr. Beck says no and they, um, keep on telling her what to do."

"If she would go back to the sea and they see things that they want to learn about Mila and the dolphins, they could just write down about the dolphins and just write the story. Maybe if, like, like if Sandy gets married in there then she could tell her kids that she had a student named Mila that was related to the dolphins and, um, so Sandy tells her children and they pass it on," Michelle remarked.

"And that's how good stories are passed on," Tim said. Then he redirected the conversation: "Let me just run one more thing by you. One of my feelings about this book is that I love it so much, I wanted to get to the end. Like Jordan, I wanted to see what happened. But at the end, I am kind of sad because, because now we won't see these characters anymore."

"You could read it over." Chris replied.

"That's right, you could read it over. That's a good point. What do you think? *Charlotte's Web* was another one of those books for me. I wanted to get to the end because I wanted to see what happened, but I was sad when I got to the end because I would never see Charlotte or Templeton or those characters in my mind again. . . . I think that is true about many, many good books. Do you share that feeling where you want to get to the end and when you do you are kind of sad because you won't see those characters anymore?" Tim asked.

Michelle shared an idea, "I know what we could do; in Mrs. Pender's class in second grade, what we did, we read Harry Potter stories, and we read two sequels, so we contacted the author and we asked questions. And maybe we could do that."

"I would like to contact Karen Hesse. For one thing, I'd like to tell her how much we liked this book. And it would be nice for you to tell her in a letter what this book meant to you. Chris was saying the other day that this was such a great book. Do you remember exactly what you said, Chris?"

"I've read lots of chapter books but this is the only important one."

"Why? Why was this an important book to you?" Tim inquired.

Chris replied, "Because, um, um, I was kind of thinking of slavery."

To clarify, Tim reacted, "How Mila was kind of like a slave? Talk about that some more."

Chris continued, "Mila was kind of a slave and Dr. Beck was like her master. Justin was like the United States who freed her.

Marcus confirmed, "I think everyone is going against Dr. Beck like slavery. Mila is like in between from slavery. Like Dr. Beck is Mila's master and Justin is the United States, freedom, or Canada, and everyone else is going against Dr. Beck. And Dr. Beck keeps saying no, no and then Justin [like the United States with slavery] gets fed up and lets her go."

Tim added, "I have to say, I feel a little for Dr. Beck. She got Mila and thought, here's a great opportunity to learn about human nature and human language; all that's a really good thing. So she sees Mila and sees a great opportunity to learn about humans."

Chris chimed in, "She's greedy."

Tim continued, "But I think she saw—it took her a while to figure it out—but she saw that Mila needed to be free. I would have liked to see the look on her face when Justin said it's time to let her go. Did she resist or did she say to herself, yeah, I agree it is time to let her go no matter what happens? Earlier in the story, she could have gone to jail if she let her go. Because Mila sort of belonged to the government, whatever that means. Remember she said she could get in trouble if she let Mila go. So I sort of felt sorry for Dr. Beck because she was stuck between two things."

Jordan commented, "I bet if she would go to jail that Justin and Sandy would probably bail her out."

Tim reacted, "Obviously all of us who know the story know it was the right thing to do to let her go, and so maybe they could have convinced the government to let her go."

Then Jordan shared a prediction she had shared earlier that didn't materialize, "When me and Mr. O'Keefe were having our written conversation, I said that, um, Mila and Justin would get married, and they didn't."

"No they didn't," Tim confirmed.

"I was hoping that they would," Jordan continued. "They would make a great couple!" Jordan exclaimed disappointedly.

And with that, Tim drew the conversation to a close, and they spent the rest of their time together after school sharing snacks and their own personal stories.

Reflecting on the Literacy Club

This conversation revealed a number of things about Tim as a teacher and about his students as readers and writers. Together they constructed and reconstructed sophisticated interpretations of this important book. In the process, they naturally learned language, learned about language, and learned through language. They also used language to critique the power structures inherent in academia in honest and sincere ways. The questions they asked reveal a respect for human dignity and concern about the ways in which research can violate it in the name of science or for the "good" of humanity at large.

The children *learned language* by reading and discussing the complex story line of this simple, elegant text. They employed strategies that allowed them to use conversations about the beginning of the book as an anchor to make sense of the dense and intense middle of the book.

They *learned about language* as they encountered the unique ways in which Karen Hesse breaks traditional writing conventions for effect. They explored the power of using poetry and prose within a chapter book format, and they learned the power of intentional decisions such as to write an entire chapter in one sentence. "I must get back to the sea" became a touchstone for the class, one that meant "breaking convention for effect." The power of language became clear for Chris and the others when he said that this was the most important book he had ever read. He was learning that language is a tool to inform, entertain, and move a reader emotionally.

These third graders learned to use *language to critique* in a number of ways. Chris's interpretation of Mila's status as a research subject being similar to slavery revealed his capacity to make profound inferences. It also made sense in light of conversations about the news and current events during morning meetings. He had recently raised issues related to slavery and civil rights when attempting to make sense of the ways in which the Taliban treated its citizens in Afghanistan and of the role of the U.S. government in the Civil War. Chris's query about the roles of the researcher and research subjects raised the issue of the potential for ethical dilemmas in such investigations. Michelle's innocent recommendation that Mila return to the sea and that Sandy "could tell her kids that she had a student named Mila that was related to dolphins" and her children could "pass it on" touched on the value of qualitative research. Michelle intuitively understood that they could learn different but incredibly valuable lessons from studying Mila in her natural environment and simply tell the story.

While there were moments of sophisticated reasoning in this conversation, it is equally important to acknowledge and value the delightful comments that third graders make. Jordan's prediction during a written conversation with her teacher that Mila and Justin would get married didn't surprise us. Personal relationships are important to Jordan, and personal relationships with happy endings are especially appealing to her. Consequently, she looked at this text through the lens of a personal theme in her life.

What about the Standards?

The Potential Hazards of Standards

Throughout our careers as teachers, we have imposed high standards on ourselves. We have also worked to address standards developed by national organizations such as the National Council of Teachers of English (NCTE) and the International Reading Association (IRA), state departments of education, and our school districts. Like so many teachers, we have been able to weave these standards into the curriculum we created with our students.

In the past fifteen years or so, however, the scene has changed. While standards once provided a broad guide for our teaching, they are now becoming a tool for control by folks outside of education. Bold and insightful educators such as Deborah Meier, Carole Edelsky, and Susan Ohanian, among others, have shown us how the push to "standardize" education through high-stakes tests and rigid standards has pushed many teachers and children out of schools. This movement has also constrained schools and teachers from doing their best, professional work. We are deeply disturbed by the deleterious effects of this sweeping movement that has changed the way many teachers and schools think about and address standards. We believe that standards were meant to help us develop comprehensive and complex curricula. Now, for many educators, standards threaten and limit both teachers and students. We are doing what we can locally to challenge this agenda and to influence the ways in which standards are developed and implemented at the local and state levels. In fact, our principal, Lyn Mueller, serves on the state English Language Arts Standards committee and is positively influencing the content, form, and implementation of the standards across South Carolina.

You have probably already concluded that Tim works in a supportive setting. In fact, Tim is encouraged to make theoretically sound decisions in his classroom. He "uncovers" standards; he doesn't simply "cover" them. He can do so because we are fortunate to be part of a school, district, and state that have been much more supportive of teachers as professionals than is the case for many of our colleagues across the country. We work in a context in which standards are used to promote good teaching.

When Standards Promote Good Teaching

The South Carolina English Language Arts Curriculum Standards and the corresponding professional development training sessions were developed in the spirit of the national standards and thus promote good teaching.

> The standards . . . define what . . . students should know and be able to do in the English language arts. . . . [W]e believe that these standards should articulate a consensus growing out of actual classroom practices, and not be a prescriptive framework. If the standards work, then teachers will recognize their students, themselves, their goals, and their daily endeavors in [them and] . . . be inspired, motivated, and provoked to reevaluate some of what they do in class. By engaging with these standards, teachers will, we hope, also think and talk energetically about the assumptions that underlie their own classroom practices and those of their colleagues. (NCTE/IRA, 1996, p. 24)

The 2002 SC English Language Arts Curriculum Standards were developed under the direction of Cathy Jones (2003), State Department of Education associate in the Office of Curriculum Standards. Cathy and her colleagues were committed to creating a set of standards that would provide support for teachers. They wanted them to empower rather than constrain good teachers, and they wanted to encourage responsive rather than formulaic teaching. Therefore, they were careful to avoid many of the recent pitfalls encountered by the standards movements in other states. They worked hard to create a set of standards that would be both theoretically sound and practically relevant. Additionally, they wanted teachers to contextualize the standards within classroom structures and strategies that reflect best practices in our field. Cathy Jones worked carefully with her team to create a matrix that would help teachers envision the relationship between particular standards in reading, writing, communication, and research and structures and strategies such as author study, guided reading, literature circles, minilessons, read-alouds, reading workshop, word study, and writing workshop (see Figure 2.7). In South Carolina, teachers are encouraged to explore and document the standards that are naturally addressed in the context of these structures and strategies. Children learn many, if not most, of the standards through repeated engagements in these practices. Teachers are encouraged to create specific demonstrations and strategy and skill lessons for the remaining standards for which students need more explicit or additional help. Clearly, this model promotes the kind of teaching that is featured throughout this book.

At the Center for Inquiry, we are frequently asked how we address the standards. While we "know" we are addressing the standards through the rich literacy experiences we create with and for our students, we also know we need to assure parents and district administrators of the intellectual rigor and integrity of an inquiry-based curriculum. As we have worked through the process of making the standards more visible without altering the nature of teaching and learning in our classrooms, we have developed a set of belief statements regarding standards. It is our hope that such statements will help others justify the ways in which they plan for and evaluate student growth in the midst of standards-based reform movements.

- Our teachers begin with intentional and systematic kidwatching. The teachers determine the ways and the order in which the standards are taught based on their assessment of children's needs and interests.

- Our teachers and children work together to uncover rather than simply cover the curriculum. In so doing, they bring the standards to life through authentic engagements, through thoughtful conversations, through interdisciplinary inquiry projects.

- Our teachers believe that the original intent of the national standards was to give teachers more power and insight, not less. So they use the standards. They don't let the standards use them.

- Our teachers organize curriculum through broad concepts or units of study that are comprehensive, not discrete. Additionally, multiple standards representing different disciplines are woven into reading, writing and math workshops day in and day out. (Mills, 2001a, pp. 218–19)

May our stance regarding the standards and the classroom examples we share throughout this book help teachers and administrators recognize the importance of uncovering standards through theoretically sound classroom structures and strategies. May it help our

**Classroom Structures and Strategies
for Comprehensive Literary Instruction
English Language Arts Curriculum Standards Connections
for Grades Three through Five**

Structure/ Strategy	Reading (R)			Writing (W)			
	Reading Process and Comprehension (1)	Analysis of Texts (2)	Phonics/Word Study and Analysis (3)	The Writing Process (1)	Writing Purposes (2)	Responding to Texts (3)	Legibility (4)
Author study							
Guided reading							
Literature circles							
Mini-lessons (reading, writing, inquiry)							
Read aloud							
Readers' workshop							
Word study							
Writer's workshop							

Structure/ Strategy	Communication (C)			Research (RS)		
	Speaking (1)	Listening (2)	Viewing (3)	Selecting a Research Topic (1)	Gathering Information and Refining a Topic (2)	Preparing and Presenting Information (3)
Author study						
Guided reading						
Literature circles						
Mini-lessons (reading, writing, inquiry)						
Read aloud						
Word study						
Writer's workshop						

Jones, South Carolina Department of Education, 2002

Figure 2.7. A page from South Carolina's English Language Arts Curriculum Standards for grades 3 through 5.

colleagues put standards into proper perspective as they develop curricula with and for children. May teachers who find inquiry-based instruction most promising find both hope and help in this text.

A Final Note

This chapter represents the structures, strategies, and daily rituals that Tim and his students have devised and embraced to nurture language, literacy, and inquiry. It illuminates the comprehensive nature of inquiry and the ways in which children learn literacy through inquiry. In the chapter that follows, we take a closer look at two individual children in order to trace their growth over time as they live and learn together in Tim's classroom.

3 Learning to See What's There

*Attending to the details of one child at a time can develop a richer under-
standing of that person, of course, and it can simultaneously strengthen a
deeper and more powerful understanding of all children, for it sensitizes
teachers to detail, to their own ability to observe and understand, and to
similarities and differences between children.*

—Ayers, 1993

Why should we include a chapter about a couple of individual
children from Tim's class? Wouldn't it be more significant to
gather stories about the entire class in order to generalize our
ideas about teaching and learning? What difference does one child or a
few children make in our ideas about how best to teach?

The short answer is that it makes a world of difference. Every child
helps us become better at our craft. Every single child who looks into
our eyes on a daily basis helps us better understand *all* children. When
we look at children as individuals, we can see beyond the class, the grade
level, and all the children we have ever taught. When we look closely
at individuals, we see humor, success, struggle, even pain. We come to
understand things about people that allow us to have compassion, to
seek to understand rather than to judge. We submit that the ability to
treat each child as an individual is what makes the difference between
a competent teacher and someone who can truly make a difference in
children's lives.

The Importance of Kidwatching

Standardized tests and other formal "objective data" give us a narrow
view of learners, one that often overlooks the everyday experiences of
a group of friends living and learning together. It would be impossible
to get to know children or to plan meaningful instruction based on this
kind of information alone. Kidwatching is a valuable alternative. It allows teachers to "know each child in as many different contexts as possible—to know each child as a person unique in all the world" (O'Keefe,
1997).

Yetta Goodman describes kidwatching as "informal observation
of the child in various situations by the classroom teacher. Since the

process itself is somewhat informal, perhaps the term 'kidwatching' is preferrable to the more formal 'observation.' Either way the process is the same" (1978). One watches children carefully in order to be a more effective teacher. Put another way, kidwatching is watching carefully and listening closely in order to provide optimal experiences for learning. We get to know children better so that we can plan with and for them.

Throughout this book we refer to Tim's note taking. This recording serves several functions. First, and perhaps most important, the act of recording notes on classroom interactions helps Tim internalize information about children. Writing down impressions simply helps him remember them. Notes, often recorded on clipboards, help Tim look for patterns in individual behavior as well as across the class. Writing conference notes across time with one child, for example, might reveal the need to suggest different genres if that child wrote about the same things again and again. Writing conference notes across the class could reveal the need to examine various kinds of prewriting strategies or to develop powerful leads. Looking closely at what children are accomplishing and what they need to work on can help teachers develop craft lessons and skill lessons.

Careful kidwatching notes help to document children's growth over time. Reading conference notes usually reveal development of more sophisticated meaning-based strategies as children mature and gain confidence as readers. Again, these observations may become strategy lessons and instructional invitations when patterns emerge.

Another important use of kidwatching data is to help keep parents informed about their child's literacy development. Whether they are records of informal conversations about kids or preparation for progress reports, kidwatching notes are valuable for their descriptions of children's growth and development. The progress reports for Jordan and Kenan presented later in this chapter came, almost directly, from notes Tim took on the reading and writing development of these two children.

Careful kidwatching means caring enough to capture the real life of the classroom—the sights and sounds of learning and teaching as it is happening, as well as reflection about classroom events after they occur. "Kidwatching provides a framework for engaging in systematic, yet very personalized, data collection in all areas of literacy" (Owocki & Goodman, 2002). This is not a chapter on kidwatching per se, although the power of kidwatching should come through as you read the stories of these two wonderful children.

Different Children, Unique Contributions

We have selected two very different children to highlight in this chapter. Although Jordan and Kenan are no longer in Tim's class, we are able to keep up with them because the Center for Inquiry is a small school. Tim sees the children during lunch, recess, carpool, and whole-school meetings twice each week. While both children are now doing very well as fifth graders, their successful paths to literacy were quite different. They enjoyed similar school experiences, yet their individual differences made their paths unique.

Jordan

During the first week of second grade, the children were a little nervous about what to expect. Most of the class had been together for kindergarten and first grade. They had spent their first two years in public school in the same classroom, with the same teacher. Jennifer Barnes was nurturing and kind, and she brought out the very best in children; the class was a tight-knit community. The kids had seen Tim before. They had spent time together during schoolwide learning celebrations and at recess and lunch, but they still felt a lot of apprehension about this new space and the new teacher.

One of the very first community-building projects Tim created was devoted to establishing the new class rules and routines. They

started with a conversation about why groups need rules; the class worked in small groups to generate ideas. When the class met to collapse their rules into a workable number, collectively they suggested many thoughtful ideas. When they had condensed the suggestions, Tim demonstrated how to shape them into a positive tone. "Don't hit," "Don't say bad words," "Don't interrupt," and "Don't yell inside," for example, became "Be kind to everyone at school. Be respectful and polite."

The class generated categories and then negotiated and agreed on the new rules. Before the document was finalized, Jordan, who had been considering the list quietly, said, "I know an important one that we missed."

"What are you thinking, Jordan?" asked Tim, who had thought the conversation had closed for the time being.

"You know how we were saying that a lot of people have a hard time saying they're sorry, and that sometimes it gets worse when people get stubborn like that? I think we should make it a rule that people should say 'I'm sorry' when they make a mistake."

"What do you think, everyone?" Tim turned the idea back to the class, quietly impressed by Jordan's depth. Everyone agreed and Jordan's rule was added to the list.

"One more thing," Jordan added when the discussion was about to come to a close again. "When a person says 'I'm sorry,' you should say 'That's all right' and forgive that person."

Rules for Living and Learning Together

Respect
Be kind to everyone at school.
Be respectful and polite.

Attitude
Have a good attitude about school.
Learn and teach as much as you can.

Effort
Always strive to do your personal best.
Use your imagination and creativity.
Use your time well.

Personal
Work out problems logically with words.
Apologize when you don't make the right choice.
Be forgiving of others.
Be supportive and inclusive.

(second-grade class, Fall 2000)

Tim had gone through this process many times, and usually the list of "Rules for Living and Learning Together" came out pretty much the same. Jordan's contributions gave the list a whole new depth and feeling. Being aware of making mistakes and taking the responsibility to make things right became an important part of the list. While the entire list was referred to countless times during the two years Tim stayed with this class, the apologizing and forgiveness rules were given special attention and reverence. These issues came up during discussions of current events (particularly the escalating conflict between Israel and the Palestinians) and the history of South Carolina, specifically the Civil War.

Tim was particularly impressed because he realized he had underestimated Jordan. The previous spring Jennifer Barnes, Jordan's first-grade teacher; Jordan's mother; the Resource teacher; the principal; and Tim had all met to help decide where Jordan's needs would be met most effectively in the 2000–01 school year. Jordan was not yet a strong reader or mathematician, and she qualified for resource assistance. Although it was suggested that Jordan have another year of first grade to give her more time to mature before going on to second grade, after extensive conversation the decision was made to let her start the year in second grade and reassess her progress the following fall.

So, even though Jordan was still an emerging reader, it became clear almost at once that she would make important, unique contributions to the class.

Kenan

Kenan came to second grade already a strong reader. His reading logs showed that he was reading lengthy chapter books, and by the end of third grade he had read *Don Quixote*. He was a fearless reader and enjoyed reading and discussing texts that were too challenging for most of his peers. But he was never a show-off about his ability. Kenan loved to learn and he saw reading as a tool for learning.

Kenan was one of those unique kids who had a strong hold on literacy and who also had the capacity to help others—his classmates and teacher and university partners—better understand the process. Early in second grade, Tim read *Thank You, Mr. Falker* (Polacco, 1998) to the class. He chose that particular book because he wanted to foster a conversation about how kids learn to read and how they should help one another in careful, supportive ways. In the midst of the conversation that followed the read-aloud, Kenan remarked, "Teachers don't make us read; they give us the courage to learn to read." In that mo-

ment, we began to realize how much we might learn from Kenan during our time together. He clearly had a solid sense of the literacy learning process. He knew his teacher could only do so much and that it was up to him to invest in learning to read and write. It was up to him to pay careful attention to demonstrations of effective reading strategies. It was up to him to make them his own. Kenan knew it was up to him to work at reading and to challenge himself as a reader. It was up to him to embrace, enjoy, and learn through literacy. And he did.

During the entire two years Kenan spent with Tim, he took every opportunity to teach and learn through literacy. In February the third-grade class was in charge of Learning Celebration. The thought for the week was "Free at Last," and the children had decided to create plays to demonstrate for the rest of the school what they had learned about the struggle for civil rights. With the entire school gathered around to watch and listen, the children acted out short plays about the Montgomery bus boycott, sit-ins at segregated restaurants, African Americans being denied the right to vote, and other examples of the Jim Crow laws. All of the dialogue, blocking, and use of props was created by the children. Tim's job was to be sure that they had the time and resources they needed to work productively on this important project.

Kenan's job was introducing one of the skits. He spoke to the school using, but not depending entirely on, the notes he wrote based on what he had learned during the focus study and his own investigations. Here is an excerpt of his introduction:

> Martin Luther King hated segregation. Segregation is when whites were kept away from blacks and blacks did not have as many rights as them. They couldn't eat at the same restaurants, couldn't drink from the same water fountains, they were treated very harsh. Martin Luther King wanted to fight back but he knew that violence wouldn't do it. He learned from Mahatma Gandhi to use non-violent methods such as sit-ins. Blacks started using non-violent methods and they worked very well. But Blacks were being treated very roughly and they were getting arrested more often. Sit-ins were when Blacks went into a whites only restaurant, they sat down and they wait to get served and, eventually they willingly got arrested. That is what this skit is about.

The school applauded Kenan's introductory piece. His succinct presentation demonstrated a great deal of understanding, and the applause was a sincere appreciation of his work and insight into the problems that faced the South before the civil rights movement. It was a perfect introduction for the play that followed about African American patrons being arrested for not leaving a white's-only lunch counter.

Similarities and Differences

While Kenan and Jordan were very different readers and writers, they both contributed tremendously to the literacy development and social consciousness of the class. Jordan had a tendency to avoid reading. During silent sustained reading (SSR), she often spent much of her time searching for a book to read rather than actually reading. Her reading logs rarely showed more than the minimum amount of time required for independent reading at home. Kenan, on the other hand, was a voracious reader. He read independently before coming to kindergarten and spent at least an hour reading at home after school every day. Kenan preferred to work by himself on many projects; he wrote the introduction to the play on his own. Jordan was very social and enjoyed learning situations in which she could choose to collaborate with her peers. She loved history, just as her parents did. Kenan was always informed about current news and world events.

Both children shared their ideas often in whole-group and small-group situations. Both shared personal connections to many topics. Jordan was concerned with the feelings of others; Kenan could be counted on to help others as a tutor on the daily math word problems. Jordan was someone the other children wanted in their author's circles for her ideas about character development and dialogue; Kenan was appreciated for his attention to detail, accuracy, and literacy conventions. Both children used written language to learn about the world.

The rest of this chapter is devoted to the lessons we learned from these very different children. The role of inquiry is explicitly demonstrated as we feature their responses to curricular invitations, and we provide "snapshots" of their literacy growth over time. Inquiry is highlighted in two parallel ways. First, you will see an inquiry-based classroom where children teach and learn in an environment meant to stimulate and capitalize on student interests, curiosities, and enthusiasms. You will also see how Tim's teacher-as-researcher stance helps him grow as a teacher as he inquires into his students' learning.

Learning through Literature Study

As mentioned in Chapter 2, during the fall of third grade the entire class read *The Music of Dolphins* by Karen Hesse for the first big literature study of the year. In this moving book, a feral child, Mila, is "rescued" from her ocean life with her dolphin family and brought to a research center to be studied by a group of scientists interested in language acquisition. Initially, Mila thrives and learns quickly how to communicate and to give the scientists what they desire. Eventually she languishes and can only think of returning to her home in the sea off Cuba with her dolphin family.

The children paired up to have written conversations as they neared the climax of the book. Some of the children wrote together in pairs. Others worked with Tim or Kimara London, the literacy assistant. Jordan worked with Tim for this engagement (Figure 3.1 is the original written version of the following conversation).

> *Tim:* What do you think Mila meant when she said that she was a "face of bones"?
>
> *Jordan:* I think she meant that Mila was looking miserable. Do you think her dreams are trying to tell her something?
>
> *Tim:* I think her dreams meant that she was afraid that she was forgetting what it was like to be a dolphin. What do you think her dreams meant?
>
> *Jordan:* I think her dreams are trying to tell her to go back to the sea or her dreams are trying to tell her that someone in her dolphin family is dying. I wonder if her dreams will come true.

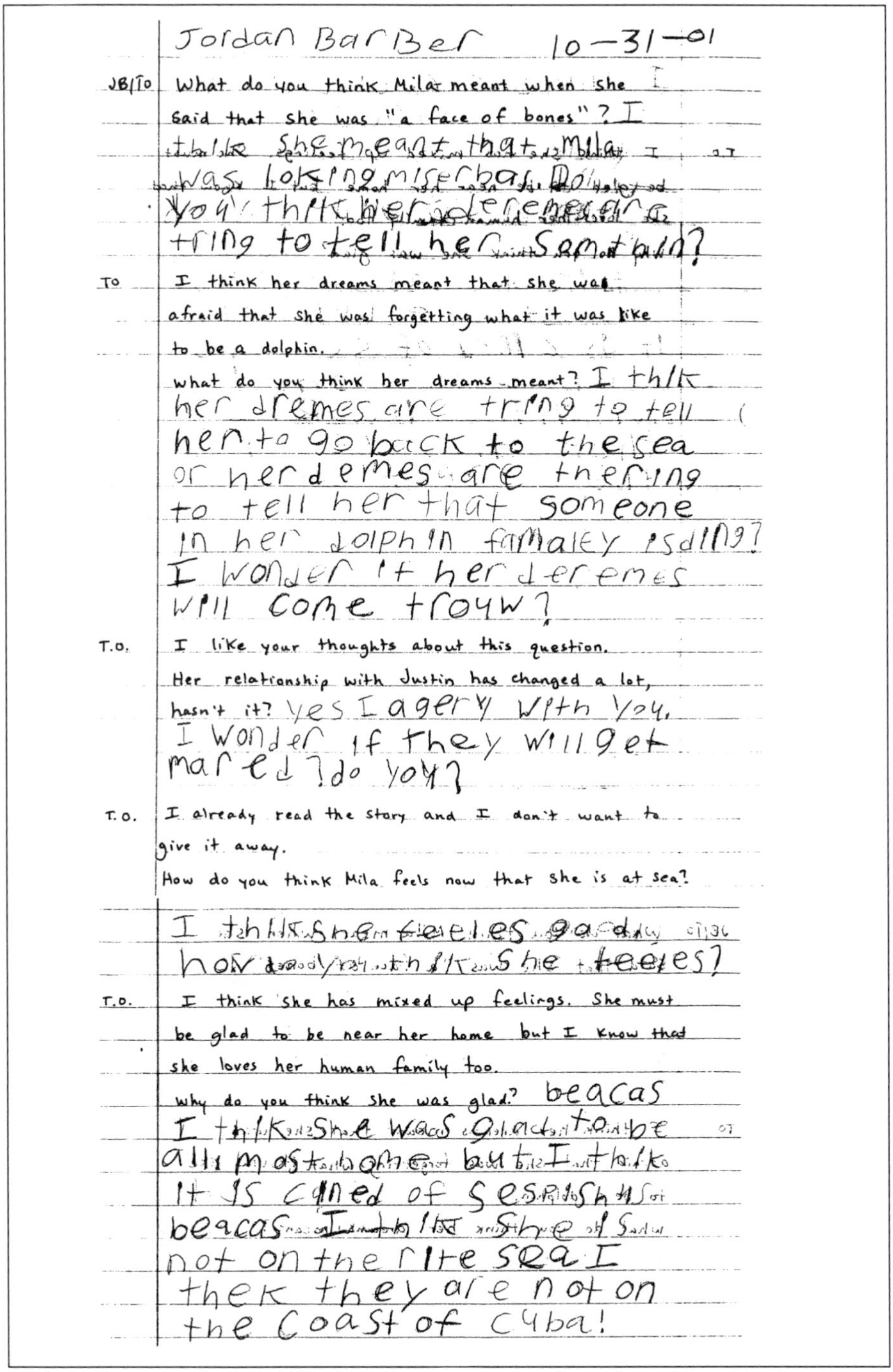

Jordan Barber   10-31-01

JB/To What do you think Mila meant when she said that she was "a face of bones"? I think she meant that Mila was loking miserbal. Do you think her demeser are tring to tell her somotpin?

To I think her dreams meant that she was afraid that she was forgetting what it was like to be a dolphin.

what do you think her dreams meant? I think her dremes are tring to tell her to go back to the sea or her demes are thering to tell her that someone in her dolphin famaley isding? I wonder if her deremes will come trouw?

T.O. I like your thoughts about this question.

Her relationship with Justin has changed a lot, hasn't it? yes I agery with you. I wonder if they will get mared? do you?

T.O. I already read the story and I don't want to give it away.

How do you think Mila feels now that she is at sea?

I think she feeles gad how dead/ry. th/ she feeles?

T.O. I think she has mixed up feelings. She must be glad to be near her home but I know that she loves her human family too.

why do you think she was glad? beacas I think she was glad to be allmost home but I think it is caned of sestash beacas I think she is not on the rite sea I thek they are not on the Coast of Cuba!

Figure 3.1. Jordan and Tim's written conversation about *The Music of Dolphins*.

Tim: I like your thoughts about this question. Her relationship
with Justin has changed a lot, hasn't it?

Jordan: Yes, I agree with you. I wonder if they will get married.
Do you?

Tim: I already read the story and I don't want to give it away.
How do you think Mila feels now that she is at sea?

Jordan: I think she feels good. How do you think she feels?

Tim: I think she has mixed up feelings. She must be glad to be
near her home but I know that she loves her human family
too. Why do you think she was glad?

Jordan: Because I think she was glad to be almost home but I
think it is kind of suspicious because I think she is not on
the right sea. I think they are not on the coast of Cuba!

Clearly, Jordan is used to having conversations about books. In
Tim's initial question, he asks Jordan to interpret a phrase: *a face of bones.*
Jordan's response shows she can go beyond the literal words to create
her own meaning: "looking miserable." Jordan's follow-up question,
"Do you think her dreams are trying to tell her something?," is also one
of interpretation. When Tim turns the question back to Jordan, she relies on her experiences with story to provide her with a rich interpreta-
tion/prediction, "to go back to the sea . . . that someone in her dolphin
family is dying." The same is true for the answer to Tim's question about
Mila's relationship with Justin, the teenage son of the lead scientist.
When Jordan wonders if the two will marry, she may be connecting to
the literary unit on fairy tales completed a few weeks earlier in which
many of the protagonists get married and live happily ever after.
Jordan's final answer also shows her strong sense of story. She links two
very different ideas: first, that Mila is glad to be almost home and second, that it is "kind of suspicious," that they might not actually be in
the right sea. Her first idea is the prediction of a successful conclusion
(as most children's books end), and the second, conflicting hypothesis
is that there might be some kind of trick involved. Jordan may have
noticed that Mila has been tricked before in the story (Mila did not know,
for example, that the door to her room was being locked for her "pro-
tection"). Or Jordan may have seen that this book is unlike other
children's books she had read in the past. There is a great deal of un-
happiness in this story and, in fact, it might just not have a happy ending after all.

Jordan came to this written conversation ready to communicate.
It was the most sophisticated book she had ever read, and she really
loved the story. Her written conversation reflects a certain passion for

the story, a connectedness with the characters. Her responses reflect the tension of characters—"it is kind of suspicious . . . I think she is not on the right sea"—as well as the mood—"Mila was looking miserable . . . she was glad to be almost home." She is comfortable making predictions and going out on a limb about the ending and clearly relies on her experiences with story to interpret and make predictions about this one.

Through her questions and responses, Jordan shows that she really does want to find out Tim's opinions and interpretations. She has some unique interpretations, which are hers alone. In this conversation, there are no shallow questions or mimicked responses, only a genuine desire to learn and share ideas.

In this piece, Jordan is a risk taker with her writing. She is willing to write what she means and not simply what she can spell. Indeed, there are many spelling miscues, but they all reflect a continuously developing set of spelling strategies that allow her to make her meaning clear and to learn language conventions while communicating through writing. She uses the word *think* eight times in this small piece. Each time she spells it "thik." Tim uses the same word four times, all spelled conventionally. Jordan writes the word *dreams* three times: *deremes,* *dremes,* and *demes.* Tim also uses the same word, twice, but Jordan doesn't access the demonstration. She is reading the words and obviously understanding them but doesn't choose to attend to the particular spellings. At this point, she is too busy communicating her ideas to attend to spelling. She is interpreting the text, enjoying the story and its possibilities, making connections to other literature, and constructing meaning. She is not just retelling what she has read and she is not using this written conversation as a spelling or grammar lesson.

Kenan teamed up with Kimara London and a classmate, Margaret, to record their thoughts about *The Music of Dolphins* (Figure 3.2 is the original written conversation, which is translated below):

> *Kimara:* Why does Mila say that the feeding tube cannot stop what is happening?
>
> *Kenan:* Maybe she's thinking it's uncontrollable. Margaret, why do you think Mila speaks the way she does?
>
> *Margaret:* I don't know but maybe because she hasn't learned to speak [or] write grammar like a two year old when they first learn to speak they don't really have "proper grammar." Why do you think that the words got bigger?
>
> *Kimara:* It's because she's reverting back to the way she was at the beginning of the book. She spoke simpler sentences and her grammar was under-developed. Why do you think Mila refers to herself as being "in the wrong room in a very big

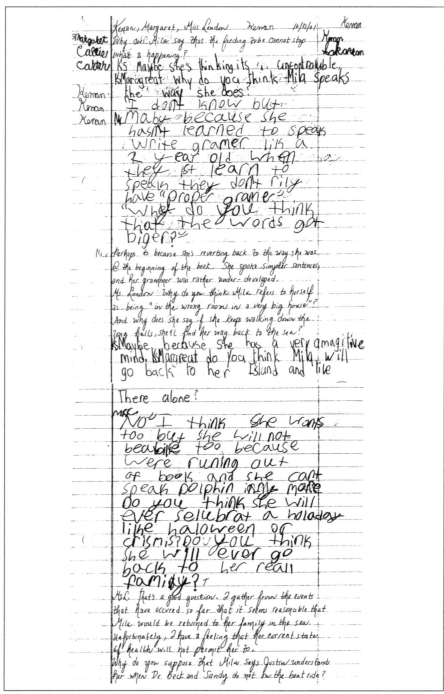

Figure 3.2. Kenan, Margaret, and Miss London's written conversation about *The Music of Dolphins*.

house"? And why does she say if she keeps walking down the long halls she'll find her way back to the sea?

Kenan: Maybe because she has a very imaginative mind. Margaret, do you think Mila will go back to her island and live there alone?

Margaret: No, I think she wants to but she will not be able to because we're running out of book and she can't speak dolphin any more. Do you think she will ever celebrate a holiday like Halloween or Christmas? Do you think she will ever go back to her real family?

Kimara: That's a good question. I gather from the events that have occurred so far that it seems reasonable that Mila would be returned to her family in the sea. Unfortunately, I have a feeling that her current state of health will not permit her to.

Kimara (Miss London) asks the children in her small group to interpret a statement ("that the feeding tube cannot stop what is happening"). Kenan's response suggests that the situation is out of Mila's control. He is taking Mila's point of view. Her health is failing, and it doesn't seem likely that the doctor in charge of her situation will let her return to her home in the sea. Kenan feels that Mila's circumstances are spiraling beyond her control. He then asks Margaret to comment about Mila's grammar. Margaret's suggestion that Mila speaks/writes like a two-year-old and that "when they first learn to speak, they don't really have proper grammar" makes perfect sense in the context of the story. When she was discovered off the coast of Cuba, Mila could not speak any human language. As Mila grows into spoken language, she reveals her language acquisition to the reader slowly, moving from large print and simple, childlike sentences to small print and complex ideas as her language develops. It is interesting to note Margaret's use of quotation marks in this sentence: "they don't really have 'proper grammar.'" Margaret's use of the quotation marks here is a sophisticated way of showing borrowed words or words used in a special way. She then overgeneralizes the use of quotation marks in her follow-up question: "'Why do you think that the words got bigger?'" She uses them again in her final answer in place of a comma: "No' I think she wants to but . . ." We find that children often overuse a convention as they begin to gain mastery of it, almost in a playful experimentation to determine specific rules.

Kimara follows with a complicated question asking Kenan to interpret two of Mila's statements. He may be hedging a little by responding that Mila has a "very imaginative mind." Kenan asks Margaret to answer the question that had come up most often in class discussions: Does she think that Mila will make it back to the sea? This is the most important and most talked-about question from the point in the book at which Mila is becoming unhappy with her life with her human family. This question weighed on the minds of the entire class. Margaret's answer reveals her previous knowledge of story form. In her opinion, Mila will not be able to get back to the sea because "we're running out of book" and there will be too many obstacles to overcome in that amount of text.

Throughout the study of *The Music of Dolphins,* Tim, Kimara, and the children were also learning language, learning about language, and learning through language. They were communicating rather complicated ideas through writing, learning the function of written language while sharing insights about this shared literary experience. They were using known conventions of written language as well as trying out new ones. All of the children were marvelous risk takers with spelling, fearlessly using what they knew about letter sounds to ask and answer questions (Jordan's *deremes, demes,* and *dremes* for *dreams;* Margaret's *gramer* for *grammar;* and Kenan's *amagitive* for *imaginative*). They were learning through language by gaining an understanding of one another's interpretations and predictions about the story. They explored tension, conflict, and the motivation of characters. At the same time, they were all enjoying the challenge of this complex book, making connections to other stories they knew and seeking out the understandings and interpretations of the others.

Literacy Learning through Science Investigations

Another example of how these children used language to record and share ideas occurred in their exploration of geology. Tim brought in various kinds of soil for the children to investigate in order to discover soil composition. On this day, the class was investigating the soil of a forest. This followed an investigation of the sandy soil of the school playground. The children were asked simply to dig into the soil and to record what they found in a systematic way. They worked at tables of three or four while Tim walked around the room also examining the soil and recording his own observations.

After a lengthy period of free exploration, the children shared what they had found in small groups and then engaged in a whole-class conversation. Kenan and Jordan sat at different tables; their observations were, of course, different too.

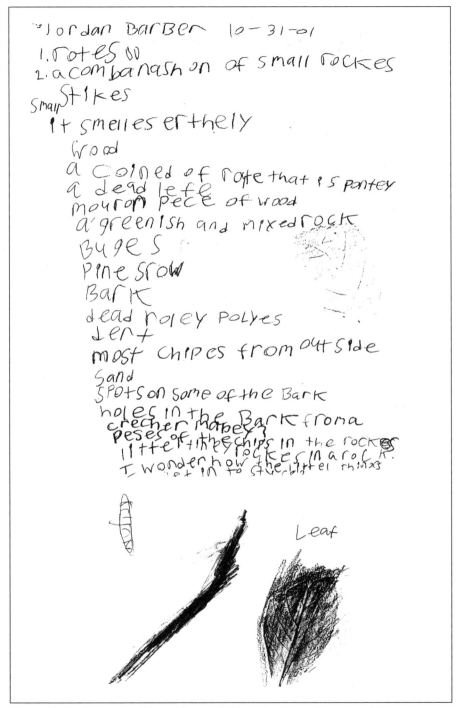

Figure 3.3. Jordan's observations while exploring soil composition.

These examples illuminate how children use writing to learn when they are asked to use what they know about language to record and share observations. Jordan's paper (Figure 3.3) is mainly a list of specific objects found in the soil (a combination of small rocks, small sticks, a dead leaf, bugs, pine straw, bark, dead roly-polies), descriptions (it smells earthy, moist chips from outside, spots on some of the bark, little tiny rocks in a rock), and questions (holes in the bark from a creature maybe? I wonder how the little things get into stuff?) While others were sketching some of their observations, Jordan made a leaf rubbing on her second sheet. This idea caught on quickly, and soon most children were doing the same thing, realizing that small details of the decaying leaves could be captured effectively. Jordan was doing what scientists often do: recording and sharing objective observations about their discoveries as well as questions generated from their observations. She wrote precisely what she found in the soil, and when she found something that she couldn't readily identify, she recorded a question to remember her thought: "holes in the bark from a creature maybe?"

Kenan created detailed sketches of creatures, roots, and a rock as well as leaf rubbings (see Figure 3.4), an idea he borrowed from Jordan. He used art in concert with writing to record a very complete set of information. The sketches provided far more information than his text alone, demonstrating his intuitive understanding of the complementary relationship between different sign systems: art and writing. His precise drawing of the root shows fine hairs extending from a larger piece. His earthworm has detailed segments, and his drawing of the isopod shows tiny antennae and legs. This attention to detail allowed him to learn even more about the complexities of forest soil. His sketches show his understanding and appreciation of the role of illustrations in nonfiction texts. Kenan's written text is mainly complete descriptive sentences: "The bark is softer when I touched it. I saw some tree cancer. . . . I took a piece of rock and it had something that looked like a fossil." He also included a list of items found on his pan of soil, including isopods, clay, things that were chewed, etc.

During this investigation, the children were all learning through language. The discussions at the tables were full of wonder and insight as the children shared exciting discoveries and careful observations. When a beetle, worm, snail, or isopod (roly-poly) was found, the announcement brought the entire class over to the table to share in the investigation. Such announcements motivated the other children to find evidence of creatures in their own soil samples. The children were using writing as a tool to assist their investigation. They shared new insights and knowledge constructed through their written responses.

Figure 3.4. Kenan's observations while exploring soil composition.

Tim found that asking the children to record observations about shared experiences before formal discussions often helped them organize and prioritize their information, making the discussions rich and full of meaning. Having their records in front of them gave them specific details from which to draw when comparing and sharing their experiences. Together, the class observation sheets, along with the conversations, left very few questions about what makes up forest soil. With twenty-two children and the teacher all contributing their findings, the question "What makes up soil?" was answered thoughtfully and thoroughly.

Writing Conferences

During most of the year, the children create their own texts during workshop. They select and experiment with different genres and topics, and they also explore different crafts uncovered during author studies, minilessons, and class read-alouds. Tim writes and publishes along with the children and records notes about the children's progress. During workshop he helps edit, forms author's circles, gets supplies, helps children create covers for their books, shares strategy lessons, and holds writing conferences. These conferences are tailored to the needs and interests of the children. This time of "checking in" is used for obtaining information about what the children are working on, checking their progress, determining what strategy lessons the class would benefit from, and coaching individual children in specific ways.

Kenan's Writing Conference, 1/29/02

Tim: Kenan, what are you working on?

Kenan: A story based on Lord of the Rings, and I made up a couple of my own characters . . . Checkapee, and it's my own idea but there's still some characters from the movie in it.

Tim: And the books too, right? Haven't you read the rest of the trilogy?

Kenan: No, I've only read *The Hobbit* and *The Two Towers* and *The Fellowship of the Ring.*

Tim: Do you mind if I have a look at your prewriting notes?

Kenan: I think they're at . . . Oh no, wait [flips to back of notebook].

Tim: I know you've written a bunch. Wow! You've got a lengthy story here. Do you have any prewriting notes or are you going pretty much . . .

Kenan: Wait. They're right here.

Tim: Great. Can you go over your prewriting notes with me?

Kenan: Well, my title is *The Last Prince.* I'm right here [points to a spot in his notes].

Tim: "Go to Rivendell."

Kenan: That's where they are in the story right now.

Tim: Where does your story start? I just want to get a sense for how far you are.

Kenan: It starts right here in Hobbiton. It got destroyed by Orcs, so now the first chapter is called "The Building of the Shire."

> *Tim:* Judging by what your prewriting notes look like, you are about halfway around your circle. How many pages would you estimate this to be?
>
> *Kenan:* I think it's eight.
>
> *Tim:* [reads for a few moments] Pretty impressive story. Thanks. I was just checking in.

In this brief two- to three-minute conference, Tim was able to see what Kenan was working on (he read a page of Kenan's text) and how much he had written (see Figure 3.5). Tim could see how Kenan used prewriting notes as a tool (Figure 3.6) and got a sense of the organization and language of Kenan's piece. Tim was also able to make connections with literature they were both interested in. It was obvious to Kenan that Tim was sincerely interested in how his story was going. Because Tim knew Kenan's history as a reader and as a writer, he could streamline the conference and was able to talk about Kenan's interests. He knew what Kenan had read over the previous year and a half from the books read together in class, as well as from Kenan's independent reading from his reading log (a daily written reflection on reading done at home). Tim knew that Kenan enjoyed writing action-packed adventures like those he often read because he took notes on everything Kenan had written and published in writing workshop.

Kenan's work on this piece amazed Tim and showed him the wisdom of allowing children the freedom to choose their own topics. Kenan had successfully cloned J. R. R. Tolkien's style but was creating a story all his own; he relied on Tolkien's characters but added some new ones (Goliath, Checkapee, and Ferard the Giant). By borrowing from Tolkien, Kenan could simply pick up where he had left off reading. By imitating the voice of this great author, Kenan himself became a stronger writer. What better writing coach could there be for a third grader than J. R. R. Tolkien? Tim also learned that Kenan had a logical plan for his writing but that he wasn't bound to that plan. This was demonstrated by the fact that Kenan didn't even know where his outline was and had to search to find it. His prewriting plan had been internalized to the point that Kenan didn't really need it in front of him. The writing had already taken on a life of its own.

Kenan's use of dialogue kept the story fast paced and interesting, *"Low, ho, ho, ho, It's a goblin's life for me,"* the voice echoed. His chapter title, "Theory in the Dark," was another way he kept his readers captivated and wanting to read on.

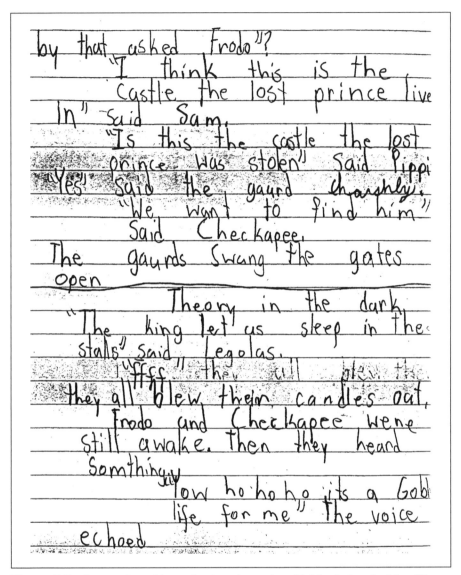

by that asked Frodo"?
"I think this is the
Castle the lost prince live
In" said Sam.
"Is this the castle the lost
prince was stolen" said Pippi
"Yes" said the gaurd charshly.
"We want to find him"
Said Checkapee.
The gaurds swang the gates
open
"Theory in the dark.
"The king let us sleep in the
stalls" said legolas.
"fff" they all blew th
they all blew their candles out.
Frodo and Checkapee were
still awake. Then they heard
Somthing.
"ow ho ho ho its a Gob
life for me" the voice
echoed

Figure 3.5. A page from Kenan's story based on Tolkien's Lord of the Rings series.

Jordan's Writing Conference, 1/29/02

Some of these conversations involved more than one student at a time. On the same day as the conference with Kenan, Tim met with Jordan, who was working on a very different story. She was sitting at a table with Jacob.

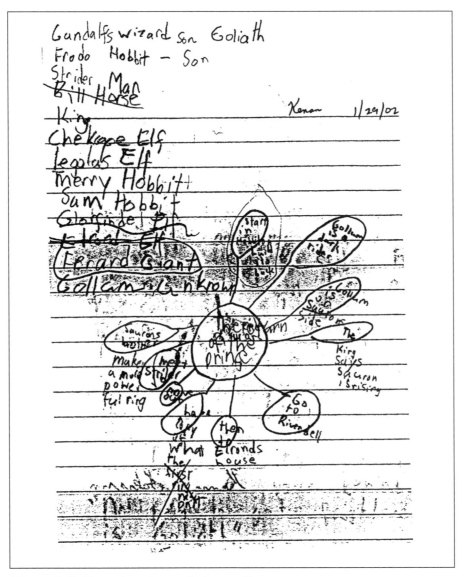

Figure 3.6. Kenan's notes and story outline.

Tim: I notice that you're writing some nonfiction and that you keep looking back and forth in your *Titanic* books. Can you tell me about what you are doing?

Jordan: Um, me and Michelle got together and we were so fascinated about the *Titanic* that we wanted to find out more about the *Titanic*. And so my mom reminded me that I had this book about the *Titanic* on my shelf, so I grabbed it from home. And when me and Michelle were at the library, we found some books on the *Titanic*, and we're going to make a report out of it. Half report, half story.

Tim: I'm not sure I know what you mean by half report, half story. It's going to have true events and there will be make-believe elements to it?

Jordan: Not really but, um, we were going to make a story out of it and make it sound like a story. Like, we're going to try to read it like a story. It's really going to be like a report.

Tim: I can't wait. So few kids write nonfiction [for workshop]. Now, Jacob, I guess it's been a few weeks now. You had that book about swords and knights and medieval times. You were using that for your story, right?

Jacob: I had four books. I got three books from the library and this book that my Aunt Sheila gave me.

Tim: So your story is going to be make-believe, but it is going to have real weapons from the time period, real artifacts?

Jordan: Yeah, he was telling me on the way to the library he was going to write a couple of books about knights and stuff because he was so fascinated and all.

Tim: And your story's different. Of course, it's a different subject, but your story is going to be entirely true. The characters in your story are going to be real people.

Jordan: Yeah, it's going to be like a story but it's going to be like a report too.

Tim: So it's going to be an interesting report that's more in the form of a story?

Jordan: Yeah. It shows here. As you can see, it has a big diagraph of the ship. [She unfolds a large diagram.]

Tim: That's huge! Four pages.

Jordan: And it shows two people and they were taking a stroll and it says their names somewhere . . . um, somewhere.

Tim: I'm proud of you for trying something like this. This would be new for the class during workshop. We do research and we do expert projects, but not many people do this sort of thing in writing workshop.

This conference was different from Kenan's. Tim validated Jordan's decision to try something new. He asked her clarifying questions to get a better understanding for himself of her writing project, and he also used his questions to help Jordan clarify for herself what she was doing. Tim drew Jacob into the conversation and made the connection between Jacob's research for his fictional stories and Jordan's research. Some of Jordan's notes were copied from the text she was reading and some came from the information she had discovered from other readings and an old folk song the class had sung together about the *Titanic* (see Figure 3.7).

Tim asked Jordan to share information about her project with the rest of the class—what she was thinking and how she was preparing to write by reading. Jordan's project became an important point of discussion about trying different genres and bringing facts to life (Portalupi & Fletcher, 2001). The idea of using story to make nonfiction interesting was one the class had already been exploring.

Tim had recently read aloud *Pink and Say* by Patricia Polacco (1994). From this story about two young boys during the Civil War, the class developed a much stronger idea of what it must have been like to live in those times. Jordan was trying to figure out how to use this strategy for herself, and the whole class benefited from her effort. In sharing her writing project, Jordan demonstrated that researching makes writing clear.

In this example, Jordan was clearly learning language by reading and writing for the purpose of communicating. She was learning about language by using nonfiction materials and content information and making it her own by creating her own historically accurate story. Jordan was learning through language while satisfying her curiosity about history in general and the *Titanic* specifically by using reading as a tool for learning and writing as a tool for communicating what she had learned.

During conferences such as these, Tim got to know all of his students well as readers and writers. Their short conversations revealed their interests, preferences, and writing styles. They also revealed a lot about what the students needed to work on in order to become more effective writers. In these brief regular chats, Tim was able to teach to children's individual needs. If children included dialogue, for example, the writing conference was a comfortable setting for direct instruction on quotation marks in the context of the child's own words. If tips about writer's craft were needed, Tim could make suggestions about planning ahead, using prewriting notes, and having an ending in mind before writing a rough draft.

Improvisation in music is an appropriate metaphor for writing conferences. Every song has a basic structure or form. It helps to be familiar with the song before reaching out beyond the melody to improvise. Knowledge of keys and appropriate chord structure is also helpful. With this knowledge of basic structure in place, a musician can play

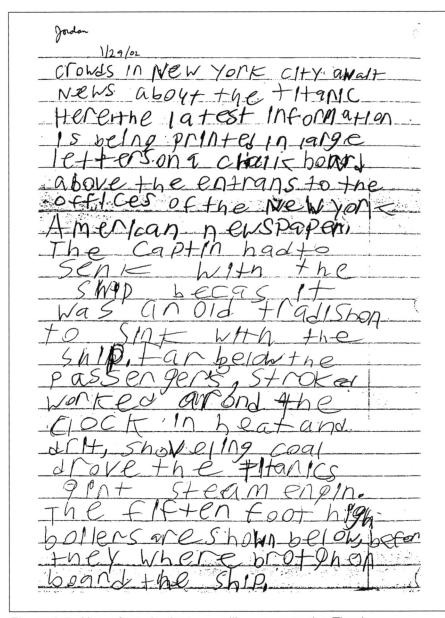

Figure 3.7. Notes from Jordan's storylike report on the *Titanic*.

the same song many times and never play it the same way twice. The solo would depend on the key, the tempo of the song, the instruments accompanying the soloist, the personality of the other musicians, the mood of the room, the enthusiasm of the audience, and, yes, past experience improvising with a particular song. Similarly, when conferencing with students, a teacher shouldn't expect to have the same conference twice.

To extend the metaphor, conferencing during workshop is responsive teaching (improvising) in its purest form. Teachers never really know what to expect other than a conversation about writing (the basic song). Connections are spontaneous, and coaching is immediate and dependent on what the child is currently thinking about (musical expressions are spontaneous and depend on the musical circumstances). Effective conferences have a lot to do with the relationship between teachers and students (the relationships between musicians). Knowledge of instructional history, reading preferences, favorite authors and genres (musical forms), as well as specific awareness of what each child needs in order to develop as a writer all contribute to the effectiveness of writing conferences. The structures and understandings are perhaps the same, but the individual circumstances are *necessarily* different, creating a unique conference (musical solo) every time.

Coaching Readers through Reading Conferences

Responding to children as writers is a challenge because thoughtful feedback depends on knowledge of each child's needs, strengths, and interests. Coaching children as readers is equally complex. While every conference promotes strategic reading habits, each conference evolves in unique ways.

Several times each year Tim sat down with the children individually and listened to them read. Most of the time the children brought the material they were currently reading to the conference. Routman (2003a) suggests this strategy as a way to get the most from reading conferences. You find out what kids are reading and whether they are making wise choices when selecting books. Additionally, they will have developed enough of a sense of the plot, characters, and setting to have a good book talk. The conference will take on depth and breadth in ways that are impossible to achieve if you always ask kids to begin with a new book you have selected.

Tim took anecdotal notes and often taped the children reading and the conversation that followed. During the reading, Tim did not interrupt or correct reading miscues. In fact, he offered assistance only when the children asked for help. He wanted them to self-correct when they realized that a miscue changed the meaning of the text. Immediately following the reading, Tim and the child discussed the text and reading strategies used (as seen in Chapter 2 with Victoria's reading conference). These coaching sessions were important in several ways. They helped Tim get to know the children as readers so that he could tailor instruction to their individual needs. They also helped him track the children's growth as individual readers and gave him information necessary to create curriculum for the entire class.

Jordan as a Reader

In mid-August of third grade, during independent reading time, Tim asked Jordan to come to his table to read. Jordan bounded over happily, carrying a copy of *A Dream Come True* (Taylor, 2000), a Rugrats book she owned. This was their first time reading together since the end of her second-grade year and both were excited. Jordan said that she had seen the Rugrats movie and that she really enjoyed it. Tim was delighted that Jordan was so enthusiastic about reading her book. He recalled that she had been a reluctant reader in second grade. Other than reading books with predictable texts, she had avoided reading aloud, even in one-on-one situations. This newfound attitude was a marked change from that of second grade.

As an emergent reader, Jordan rarely self-corrected miscues even when it was clear they didn't make sense in the context of what she was reading. Her strategies were inefficient in that she relied so heavily on sounding out words that she sounded like she was reading a list of words rather than a story. Throughout second grade, Tim stressed that reading was about *making sense* of text by using a balance of cueing systems (semantics, syntax, and graphophonemics). Common strategy lessons included cloze (a strategy in which readers fill in deleted words, encouraging a focus on context to make meaningful predictions), sketch-to-stretch (representing the meaning of a reading through art), and written conversations (conversing with a partner on paper) to share ideas about stories and reading logs (Short & Harste, 1996; Fountas & Pinnell, 2001). Comprehension-focused conversations about stories were central to shared reading experiences. Together, the class created a lengthy list of reading strategies that was continually updated as new strategies were explored. These were prominently displayed in the room and revisited frequently. Still, Jordan remained a reluctant reader who avoided reading altogether.

Now, as she came up to Tim's table, Jordan had a sly smile on her face, as if she had a secret she couldn't wait to share. Tim switched on the tape and Jordan said that she had a new book she really liked. This alone was an important change in Jordan, since she had never been very enthusiastic about any book except read-alouds. "It's called *A Dream Come True.* It's a Rugrats book. I saw the movie this summer. Did you see the movie?"

Tim said that he had seen the movie with his family and that they all liked it a lot. Jordan seemed genuinely happy for the opportunity to share the new book with her good friend, her third-grade teacher.

She opened the book, tucked a strand of hair behind her ear, and started reading aloud. She read the first two sentences slowly and carefully, sounding a little stilted and word-for-word. As she read the third sentence, she came to the name of a character, Stu. Jordan read, "Tommy's dad *stood* . . ." She glanced down at the picture and reread the sentence, self-correcting her miscue. "Tommy's dad, Stu, had been asked to fix a Reptar he had designed for Reptarland there." Tim, who was recording anecdotal notes for this reading sample, noted that Jordan had made a miscue but then self-corrected when she noticed that it didn't make sense. Tim was quietly surprised and pleased that Jordan was attending so closely to the meaning of the story that she caught the miscue herself. While this wasn't the first time Jordan had self-corrected, it was certainly rare in his experiences with her.

As she read on, Jordan began to use effective intonation in her voice, indicating that she was attending to punctuation and the different characters' voices. She was beginning to read fluently. Jordan came to the word *introduced* in the sentence *Then Angelica introduced the babies.* She began "in . . . indiscuss . . . in . . . intruh . . ." Tim asked her to read on and to come back to the word with more clues.

After she had read the rest of the sentence, Tim asked, "What would make sense there?"

"Introduced!" Jordan exclaimed as she realized she had read the sentence all by herself. "She *introduced* the babies!"

Reading on, Jordan said "troll brother" for *drooly brother.* She did not self-correct then, perhaps because Jordan knew Angelica's character well enough to realize she was probably insulting Baby Dil in her introduction and *troll* was an insult that worked for her. Tim noted the miscue but had a hunch it wasn't one that changed the meaning of the story.

A few sentences later the Angelica character asks someone if she speaks French. Her answer in the text is, *"Oui, yes!"* Jordan read, "Oh! Yes!" Tim was recording that the miscue did not change the meaning of the piece when Jordan said, "I have a feeling that doesn't say 'Oh.'"

Tim said there would probably be more French words in the book since it was set in France. "That word is *oui;* it means 'yes.'"

Jordan inquired, "Why would they write 'Yes, yes'?"

"I'm not sure, Jordan. Maybe the author is trying to teach us some French." As she read on, Jordan did make some miscues that changed meaning ("gill—gear—gans" for *gigantic* and "man-sprinted" for *mean-spirited*). But she clearly understood the text in general and, beyond that, really seemed to enjoy the story. She smiled at the funny parts, made spontaneous comments about the characters, and shared that the book was "almost exactly like the movie except the movie had more stuff in it." At one point in the text, the twins, Phil and Lil, were described as *bookends*. Jordan misread "boogers" and, with a chuckle, self-corrected. Near the end of her reading sample, Jordan read "said" for *shouted*, a miscue that clearly did not change the meaning of the sentence. She read on, maintaining the rhythm and flow of the story.

When Jordan returned to her pillow for more independent reading time, Tim wrote the following in his notes:

> Impressions: J is becoming a more thoughtful, conscientious reader, noticed several miscues which changed meaning, lots of self-correcting (!), lots of smiles, good general understanding (of course she knows the movie), chatty, more confident, just right book for her. Are there other Rugrats books out there? Books from movies or TV shows, or ones she has heard read aloud might be good for her. Big change!

Jordan had made a huge leap in understanding what she was reading. In previous reading samples, she did not seem to monitor her reading for meaning; she rarely self-corrected in second grade. Tim knew there would be no turning back for her now that she was enjoying reading. As he implied in his notes, Tim realized that part of his job now would be finding appropriate reading materials for Jordan and keeping careful watch on her progress. He would look carefully at her reading logs and maintain close contact with Jordan's parents to celebrate her recent accomplishments. He would make sure she had plenty of books available to practice reading independently. Jordan had crossed an important threshold. She was reading for meaning. Although Jordan had arrived at this point later than many of her peers, it was clear that she was on the right track—that she was a new member of the Literacy Club (Smith, 1981).

Kenan as a Reader

Reading conferences take a lot of time. In order for the teacher to get an effective sample, the child must read for several minutes and have the opportunity to talk about the story. Finally, the coaching portion of the interaction must be customized to the individual child. Like writing conferences, reading conferences are as unique as the children involved. For Jordan, Tim's coaching focused on being sure she was using a balance of cueing systems to construct meaning. He helped her to define reading as making sense. For Kenan, Tim's coaching was very different.

Kenan was reading one of C. S. Lewis's The Chronicles of Narnia books, *The Magician's Nephew* (1955). He was just beginning the book and had already read a few of the other books in the series. He was excited about this book because he was so fond of the others he had read, and he wanted to begin reading right away. Tim knew that Kenan was a fast reader and that it would probably take him only a few days to finish the entire book.

While working with Tim, Kenan read quickly and made very few miscues that changed the meaning of what he was reading. He did mispronounce some proper nouns, such as "Barnstables" for *Bastables*, "Lewiston" for *Lewisham*, and "Effton" for *Eton*. Such miscues made very little difference in constructing meaning for this young third grader. Kenan's substitutions for these proper nouns looked and sounded similar to the names from the story and functioned exactly the same way.

A little further on Kenan read, "After you've been bubbling," for the words *"After you've been blubbing."* Kenan paused and reread this phrase, this time pronouncing *blubbing* correctly. "I sure don't know what that means. Do you, Mr. O.?" he asked, genuinely perplexed. Tim shared his confusion.

"Maybe we could look it up," said Kenan.

"Let's read on," Tim suggested. "Maybe we'll figure it out."

Kenan shrugged and read on, "'*All right, I have then,' said Digory in a much louder voice, like a boy who was so miserable that he didn't care who knew he was crying.*"

"Ah, it means crying," said Kenan, proud of this discovery. "It kind of sounds like *blubbering*." They agreed that *crying* would be the best substitution for the word, and Kenan kept reading. In the minutes that followed, Kenan made only a few miscues ("Miss" for *Mr.* and "He" for *She* and "his dried" for *dried his*), and all of these he self-corrected. A few times he reread a word or phrase, but he did so in ways that did not detract from the flow of the story.

When Kenan closed the book, he and Tim began debriefing. Kenan noticed changes in his reading and mentioned that he was trying to develop his reading vocabulary. When Tim asked how he did that, Kenan replied, "Well, I read challenging books, and when I need to, I look up words in the dictionary."

"When you stop in the middle of your reading and look up a word, doesn't that interrupt the flow of the story for you?"

"Well, it sort of does, but I can handle it,' Kenan replied, seriously.

"I'll bet you can," Tim smiled. "But you were able to figure that word out without looking it up, weren't you?"

"Yes, but I don't know *exactly* what it means."

"I'll bet you do," said Tim, quietly impressed by Kenan's self-awareness as a reader. "Why don't we look it up to be sure." After looking up the word *blubbing* in two dictionaries, the two could not locate the word.

"Well, it's got to mean 'crying.' It kind of said so right in the story."

"That's true," said Tim. "And we didn't really need a dictionary to figure that out. I think it's a great idea to look up words to develop your vocabulary, Kenan. But when you are right in the middle of reading and you don't want to interrupt the story by looking up a word, sometimes I think it's okay to just read on. Sometimes it doesn't make that much of a difference, but a lot of the time you can figure out what the word means by reading the meaning of the sentences around it. Using the context, you know?"

Next, Kenan and Tim talked about other books in The Chronicles of Narnia series. They talked of C. S. Lewis and J. R. R. Tolkien and the movies that had been made from their books. When Kenan returned to his seat, where he preferred to read, Tim wrote in his anecdotal notes:

> Impressions: K. is a fantastic reader! He reads so often and such challenging books. I am pleased with his vocabulary development. He's so aware of his strengths and what he needs to do to become a better reader. Discussed using the context to figure out new words as an alternative to always looking things up. Great short book talk about C. S. Lewis, Tolkien and films. Awesome!

Reading conferences for these two children were very different. They *needed* to be because these two readers needed very different things. Jordan needed to be validated for her growth toward meaning making in reading. This was obviously a huge step for her—reading was no longer just saying words or cracking the code. She clearly understood that reading is a process of understanding, interpreting, and connecting. Jordan had reached a new level of enjoyment and involvement in her reading, and Tim reinforced that by encouraging her to reread everything that didn't make sense. Jordan knew that Tim was proud of her development. She and Tim laughed about the antics of the characters and found common ground because both had seen the movie from which Jordan's book was made.

Kenan, already a confident and competent reader, needed to have a book talk, to share his excitement about C. S. Lewis and make connections to other authors and to film. Tim's coaching was a suggestion for a slight variation in Kenan's approach to vocabulary development. Tim assumed that Kenan didn't stop very often to look up words in the middle of his reading; he never noticed Kenan getting up during independent reading time to look up words. By coaching Kenan to use the context to figure out unfamiliar words, Tim assumed that he was merely reinforcing Kenan's expertise with this strategy.

Snapshots of Two Learners

To truly learn about children and classroom interactions, one must look at a series of events over time. Single stories and samples can demonstrate a great deal but never quite show the entire picture. Even several stories over two years don't yield a definitive look into literacy development. Questions always remain about what motivated a child to write something, when a certain skill or strategy was learned, what the day-to-day sequence of events was that led children through the pathways to literacy. If you are a classroom teacher, you know that children do not learn reading and language mechanics in the same sequence. In fact, very few children learn in the order suggested by scope-and-sequence skills charts in most reading and language arts textbooks.

Children come to us each fall so very different from one another. Their unique qualities come from previous literacy experiences, instructional histories, family lives, preferences, pet peeves, and so forth. Even very young children with no prior school experience step into their first preschool or kindergarten classroom with well-developed notions of literacy. Some have been read to since they were born. Others have had very few experiences of being read to. Some children have been encouraged to take risks with writing and come to school confident and eager to learn to write. And of course some children have been told from the first time they picked up a crayon or a pencil that they don't know how to write and that what they are writing is entirely wrong.

Jordan and Kenan were in many ways very different learners, even though they had been in the same class since kindergarten and had had essentially the same literacy engagements in school. They heard the same books read aloud, had the same amount of independent reading time in school, researched for presentations at the same time, and wrote pen pal letters to the same classes. Yet their pathways to literacy were different.

Figure 3.8. Jordan's contribution to the first-grade class Halloween book.

This being said, both Jordan and Kenan became strong readers and writers in their own fashion and at their own pace. In this section, we fast-forward through the children's literacy growth, providing glimpses from grade 1 through grade 3. Since Tim was with this class for grades 2 and 3, he was able to participate in the remarkable growth of these two charming children.

Jordan: A Gallery

Just after Halloween in first grade, Jennifer Barnes, Jordan's teacher, asked all the children to contribute to a class book about what everyone dressed as for Halloween. Each child drew what he or she looked like in his or her costume and wrote about the character portrayed. Jordan's contribution is featured in Figure 3.8. Translated, this reads:

I was Cinderella. I went to the ball. I lost my slipper. I married the prince.

From this piece of writing, it is obvious that Jordan was encouraged to take risks with writing. She knew that the function of writing was to record meaning, and she did so simply and clearly. She was learning language while leaving her thoughts behind for others in the class to read. Her first letter covered two lines. She had already written "I YS" (I was) and then erased it in favor of the larger capital *I*. Perhaps she was creating an illuminated first letter as in so many of the stories that had been read to her. Maybe she simply intended to write everything in a great large font and then abandoned this strategy in favor of letters half as big. Whatever her reason, it seems intentional, because she erased her first attempt in favor of the giant *I*.

In this piece, Jordan demonstrates fairly good use of letter sounds. While Jennifer didn't teach letter sounds in isolation, she did take opportunities to help children use them in their own writing. Jennifer may have helped Jordan learn about language while helping her sound through some of these words, but this piece clearly belongs to Jordan. In the word *Cinderella,* she did a nice job of saying the word slowly to herself and writing down the letter sounds she heard in the word. Recording seven letters and their corresponding letter sounds for this four-syllable word demonstrates strong phonemic awareness. Jordan was still mixing capital and lowercase letters, but by this time she had a good notion of "wordness," leaving fairly consistent spaces between most words. She also wrote one complete sentence per line and ended each with a period.

Although Jordan was making progress in the early months of second grade, Tim was concerned about her attitude toward reading. Jordan avoided it, and Tim knew that unless she could develop more positive feelings about reading, her path toward literacy would be a long and difficult one. He noted this and other concerns and accomplishments in Jordan's first narrative progress report in second grade (see Figure 3.9).

As part of the evaluation process, each child was asked to fill out a student self-evaluation form. Jordan's was hastily done and did not reveal much about her growth during the first nine weeks of second grade (Figure 3.10).

In second grade, Jordan contributed frequently to the large public journals for language, math, science, and culture. Jordan was more interested in the science journal than the others, although she contributed to all of them. These were truly informal places to record thoughts

Center for Inquiry
Progress Report 2000–2001
Richland County School District Two & University of South Carolina *Small School Partnership*

Student:	Jordan Barber
Teacher:	Tim OKeefe
Grade:	2
Assigned to grade:	
Grading period:	XX

Child's Growth as a Reader:
Working with Jordan in reading is challenging. She is a reluctant reader and avoids reading when she can. She is willing to read to me and enjoys reading with friends. She reads at home for the reading logs and I can tell from her writing and drawings that she is benefiting from this time spent reading. She does not use her independent reading time very well and I have changed the routine for her to include some time to read with others to be sure that she spends more time reading. Id like to see her increase the time she spends reading at home to at least 20 minutes a day. Reading to her and discussing stories will help a lot and should be enjoyable. Taking dictation and writing stories with her will help in that these may become good reading materials for her (such as the fairy tale we wrote together in our literacy club). My goal for Jordan is for her to become more independent with reading this next nine weeks and for her to simply spend more time reading.

Child's Growth as a Writer:
Jordan is a willing writer and a good risk taker. When she is motivated and stays on task she can be very productive. She isn't using conventions consistently yet (capitalization, punctuation and spelling) but she has an interesting writing voice. In a letter to my mom she wrote, thak you for the caer pak. Thea Work nisLe. I Love MynWut was Mr. Okef like Wen he was LeTul. (Thank you for the chair pack. They work nicely. I love mine. What was Mr. O'Keefe like when he was little?)

Child's Growth as a Learner in General:
Jordan is a very friendly and active child. She is a great conversationalist and contributes a lot to class discussions about read aloud books, current events, and common experiences. She lacks confidence in many academic areas, which seems to prevent her from applying herself. Instead of seeing reading as a challenge, she avoids it, which slows her progress. The same can be said about math. I see some development in her concentration but there is a lot of room for growth in her willingness to meet challenges head on. She is curious and enjoys active learning. She is definitely at her best when she is being creative and moving around the room. She is helpful when there is an opportunity to clean up the room or organize an area. She is funny and has a great sense of humor. She gives positive feedback to her peers in their work presenting or reading their books to the class. Jordan can be a better student by paying close attention to instruction, asking questions about things that she has a hard time under-standing and simply trying her best. I appreciate all that you do at home to reinforce what we do in school. Jordan is a neat kid.

Figure 3.9. Tim's first second-grade narrative progress report for Jordan.

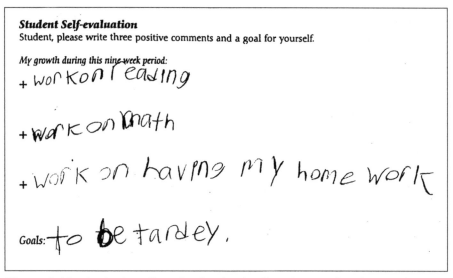

Figure 3.10. Jordan's self-evaluation for the first nine weeks of second grade.

until the next morning meeting, when the students could read their ideas and explain their insights and questions to the class, generating conversation about a wide range of topics. One of Jordan's language journal entries read (see Figure 3.11):

I can count English and Spanish.

Jordan and her classmates usually wrote in the journals quickly and did not focus as much on conventions as they did with other writing invitations such as literature responses or pen pal letters. These journals served as a record of ideas and conversations; they were not intended to be edited or rewritten. Although this journal entry was written nearly a year after Jordan's contribution to the class Halloween book, it does not have the carefully considered letter-sound correspondence of her piece about Halloween. Still, she did spell three of the six words conventionally. Her choice of letter sounds to represent the other three words (*caent* for *count*, *inglesh* for *English*, and *spanesh* for *Spanish*) demonstrates that she was attending to this structure. Writing *ing* for the first syllable in *English* indicates that she did attend to the minilesson about this suffix and simply overgeneralized it to fit the same sound in another word.

Jordan did not use a period at the end of the sentence and did not write in straight lines. The journals were made of blank white paper and did not have lines to guide the children's handwriting. Jordan

Figure 3.11. One of Jordan's language journal entries from second grade.

had a tendency to write very large in these journals. In this piece, she ran out of space, so she had to curve her writing downward in order to fit in her idea, which collided with her name. It is interesting to note that she self-corrected the backward *p* in the word *Spanish*. Jordan was monitoring her writing and, like so many children at the beginning of second grade, she was working through the direction of *B*s and *D*s, *P*s, *Q*s, etc. This is another example of learning about language while learning through language.

This little piece demonstrates that language learning is definitely recursive, not a linear process. So much of children's focus on writing mechanics depends on the context surrounding the event. In this case, the note in the language journal was a memo to Jordan herself. She used the journal as a memo pad to initiate a conversation with her peers. In all of her journal entries, Jordan was learning the function of language (learning language) while she was using her knowledge of language conventions (learning about language). At the same time, Jordan was learning through language inasmuch as she was using her writing as a

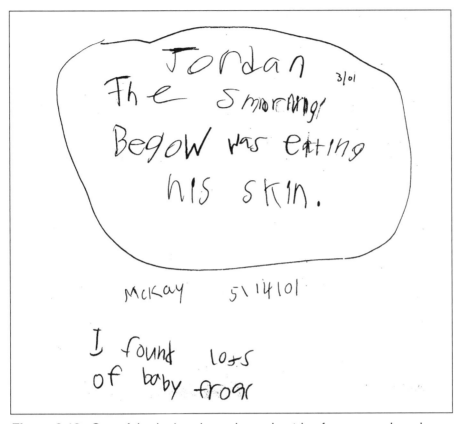

Figure 3.12. One of Jordan's science journal entries from second grade.

tool for communicating her knowledge. In this case, she was communicating her knowledge of Spanish. After reading this piece to the class, Jordan did count to ten in Spanish, much to the satisfaction of her classmates.

> This morning Bingo was eating his skin.

In a science journal entry she made a few months later (Figure 3.12), Jordan was describing the class pet African water frog's habit of occasionally eating his old shed skin. Several of the children witnessed the event, but it was Jordan who decided to record it in the science journal. She did this to inform other children who had not been there to see this fascinating occurrence. Jordan read her entry matter-of-factly at the morning meeting, and a brief discussion followed about why so many animals ingest their old skins. Children connected to other observations about tiny caterpillars the class had collected eating their eggs. Once again, Jordan was learning language, learning about language, and learning through language while she focused the class on this interesting animal behavior.

In this piece, Jordan capitalized correctly, her handwriting was linear, she used a period at the end of her sentence, and four of the seven words were spelled conventionally. The word *morning* is actually spelled correctly, but somehow the *s* from *This* was moved over into the next word. Her handwriting is smaller than in the piece in the language journal, and she self-corrected at least three times. She changed the *t* in her first word from lowercase to capital, rewrote the word *morning* more conventionally, and changed *eting* to *eating*. While she missed the *ing* sound in the word *Bingo*, she made more of an effort to write conventionally, or at least it took less effort to do so, indicating that Jordan was internalizing many language structures over the course of these few months.

By the end of second grade, Jordan was developing into a more careful writer and a more willing reader. This was reflected in her anecdotal progress report from the end of the third nine-week period (see Figure 3.13).

On the first day of third grade, Tim asked the students to write and draw about themselves for the large bulletin board, which was currently blank and covered only with bright yellow chart paper. Tim used the bulletin boards and wall space for the children to display their own work, such as projects they were currently working on, their pieces reflecting current units of study, and class-created decorations. All but a few of the children in the class were returning from the previous year, so the writing began at once. The invitation was to "write about yourself so that anyone who comes in and reads your piece will know a lot about you."

There was little hesitation to write among the returning students, although their writing did appear a little rusty from the many weeks of vacation. Jordan took just a few minutes to fill an entire page (see Figures 3.14 and 3.15).

> I like roller coasters.
> I love school
> I went to Carowinds.
> I love reading.
> I went to the beach and saw the Blue Angels.
> I have a dog named Spanky.
> I am going to Tampa for a wedding in October.
> I love macaroni and cheese.
> I love Backstreet Boys.

Center for Inquiry
Progress Report 2000–2001
Richland County School District Two & University of South Carolina *Small School Partnership*

Student:	Jordan Barber
Teacher:	Tim OKeefe/Travis Williams
Grade:	2
Assigned to grade:	
Grading period:	1

Child's Growth as a Reader:
I have been amazed in these several months by Jordan's growth as a reader. One plus for Jordan is that she is paying more attention to what she is reading and making meaning from text. Jordan should continue to think about reading strategies such as coming back to a word, and using context cues to help her. Jordan has developed tremendously as a reader this year. Her attitude about reading has developed as much as any child in our room. She no longer avoids reading as she has in the past and now often asks to read aloud to the class! She still has difficulty reading material that is considered to be grade level but her development has been truly wonderful this year. I enjoyed her book talk. She was well prepared. I could tell that she had practiced the book and she read it very well.

Child's Growth as a Writer:
Jordan is adding more details to her writing. Her slave story had a lot of dialogue and painted a very clear picture. I would encourage Jordan to try to publish more often. I continue to be impressed by the quality of her writing. She writes quickly and meaningfully, sometimes not attending much to conventions. She has no difficulty putting her thoughts down on paper. When I ask her to read over what she has written, she can identify and correct many of her own miscues.

Child's Growth as a Learner in General:
Jordan is a hard working child who has grown a lot this school year. Her strength is her enthusiasm to learn and to share what she has learned, although I continue to have areas of concern for Jordan academically. Her attention during instruction is developing but there is still a lot of room for growth in this area. Jordan is funny and cooperative, kind and very friendly. She is much better at completing assignments and her homework is done much more carefully than earlier this year. She is a sensitive child and a good friend. It is a pleasure being her teacher.

Figure 3.13. Tim's anecdotal progress report for Jordan from the end of the third nine-week period of second grade.

> I love Harry Potter.
> My family goes to the beach.
> I have a sister named Kristen.
> My mom is a nurse and my dad works for the archives and history.
> I love fireworks.
> I love ice cream.

Figure 3.14. Jordan's self-portrait at the beginning of third grade.

My best friend is Allie and Elizabeth and Kylie.
I love to sing.
I love to ride my bike.
I love animals.
I love Nintendo.
I have a Gameboy.
I love the pool.
I love the lake.

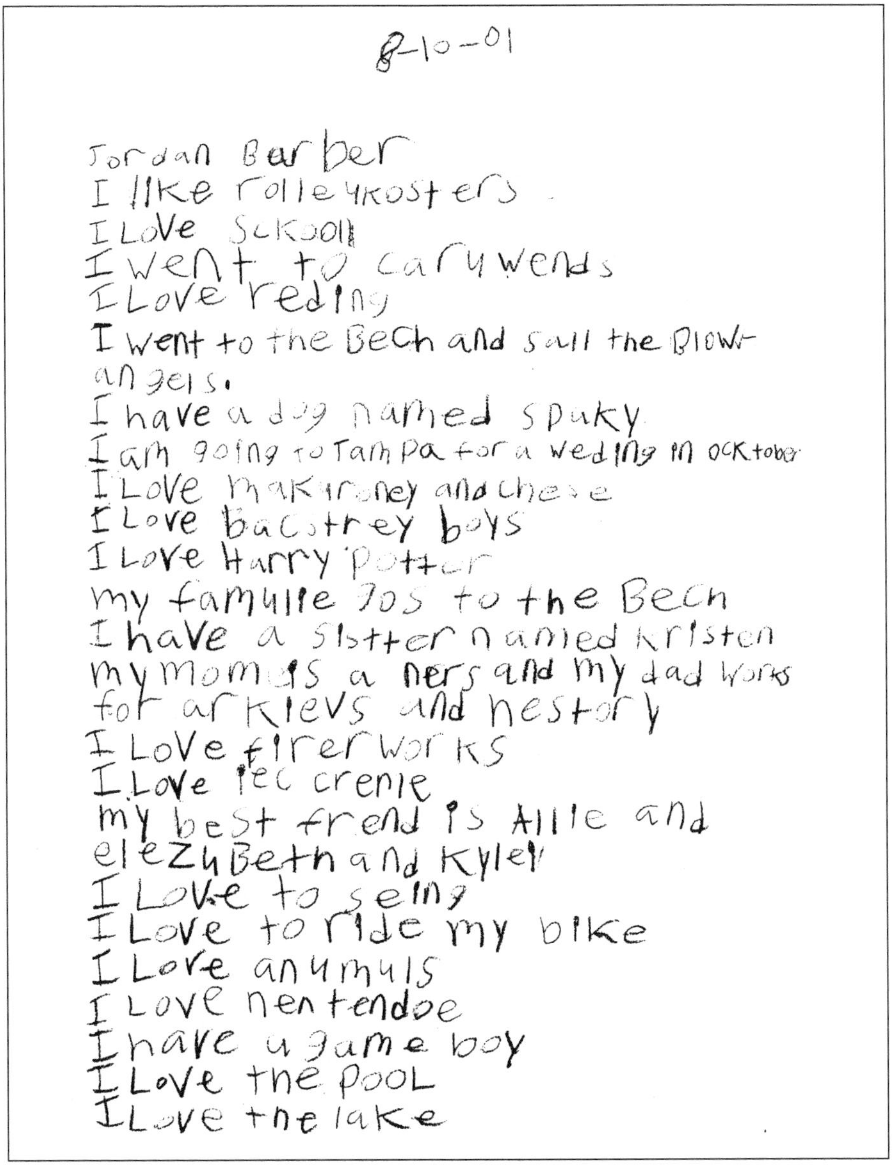

8-10-01

Jordan Barber
I like rolleykosters
I Love sckooll
I went to caruywends
I Love reding
I went to the Bech and sall the Blow-
angels.
I have a dog named spuky.
I am going to Tampa for a weding in ocktober
I Love makironey and chese
I Love bacstrey boys
I Love Harry Potter
my famulle Jos to the Bech
I have a sbtter named kristen
my mom is a ners and my dad works
for arkievs and hestory
I Love firerworks
I Love iec crenie
my best frend is Allie and
elezybeth and kyley
I Love to seing
I Love to ride my bike
I Love anumuls
I Love nentendoe
I have a game boy
I Love the pool
I Love the lake

Figure 3.15. Jordan's list in response to the invitation to "write about yourself so that anyone who comes in and reads your piece will know a lot about you."

Jordan fulfilled Tim's request to tell a lot about herself. This long list of likes and loves paints an accurate picture of Jordan's life at this time. She didn't intend to write an autobiography or a narrative—she intended to write a list. Within this list, Jordan wrote about her family

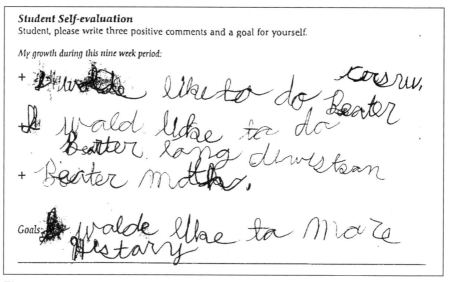

Figure 3.16. Jordan's self-evaluation for her second progress report of third grade.

(including her dog Spanky), her musical preferences (Backstreet Boys), favorite family vacation spots, and what she thinks about school, best friends, and so on. Her list is succinct and accurate.

In this piece, Jordan did not pay much attention to many of the writing conventions she had previously demonstrated in second grade. She used one punctuation mark, a period at the end of her fifth sentence. Her capitalization is inconsistent and, while her spelling is readable, it does not reflect the care she gave to many writing projects completed several months earlier. Jordan would take much more care in writing about herself later in the year.

That fall the children learned to write in cursive. Jordan was excited about this and adopted cursive for most of her writing from about November on. It was a challenge for her, but Tim appreciated her effort. She erased a lot when her writing wasn't as neat as she wanted it, and she often wrote over letters or words as she self-corrected. Being able to write in cursive was so important to Jordan that she included it on her self-evaluation, which accompanied her second progress report (see Figure 3.16):

> I would like to do cursive better.
> I would like to do better long division.
> Better math.
> I would like to [study] more history.

It is a little difficult to figure out spelling miscues when reading Jordan's cursive from this period. Some words that look like spelling miscues may be due to the formation of cursive letters (such as the way Jordan wrote the letter *a*). At first this slowed her down, and she simply did not write as much as she had written before. So much of her effort went into looking up at her cursive writing chart and rewriting for legibility that her writing voice became obscured. Even when she could have written in manuscript, Jordan chose to keep working at cursive. While her writing remained functional, Jordan had temporarily lost some of her fluency.

Within a month, Jordan was able to write more quickly and easily and had regained her voice as a writer. In mid-February, Tim asked the children to write about themselves again, this time a short autobiographical piece for student-led conferences. The invitation was the same as on the first day of school. The children were asked to use the prewriting techniques they had been developing in workshop to prepare for their pieces. Jordan chose a semantic web (Figure 3.17) and followed it closely in writing about herself (Figure 3.18). The students' rough drafts were edited and rewritten in final draft form.

> My age is 8 years old. I like to play soccer and I am on a soccer team. I acolyte at my church and help my church. My favorite food is macaroni and cheese. I like to read ghost stories and other things. My best friends are Allie Showalter and Elizabeth Basnight. I can roller skate. I like to play Frogger and spend time with my family. My goals are to do better in math. I love to go to Chuck E. Cheese and play with my friends. I have been to Disney world for vacation. I was born in South Carolina. I have a dog. His name is Spanky. I am in the third grade at the Center for Inquiry. My dad works for Terminix and my mom is a nurse and my sister is in first grade and goes to the same school.

The children took time during preparation for their student-led conferences to look over their portfolios, select representative pieces of their work, and reflect on their growth on a response form. Jordan compared her writing sample from August of third grade (Figure 3.15) to the one she had just finished (Figure 3.18). She considered these pieces as well as her entire portfolio in her reflection about her growth as a writer (Figure 3.19).

> When I was little I thought that scribble scrabble was the way to write. And now I know that there are things called manuscript and cursive. I always thought that I would be a good writer and I was right. Now I write good stories.

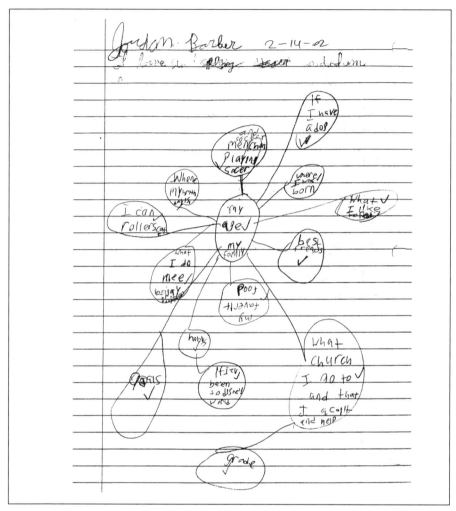

Figure 3.17. Jordan's semantic web in preparation for autobiographical writing.

Jordan was right. She did become a good writer. Her latest autobiographical piece was thoughtful and demonstrated growth as a writer.
Not only did she successfully adopt cursive, but she also carefully considered her words. She had a plan and she used it to create a piece of
writing just as revealing as the one she had written in August. In some
ways, this also was a list of favorites, but her voice comes through in a
natural, narrative tone. It is obviously more conventional. Although the
final draft was edited, the words remained Jordan's. Her recent control
of cursive, which had slowed her down for a while, served her well.

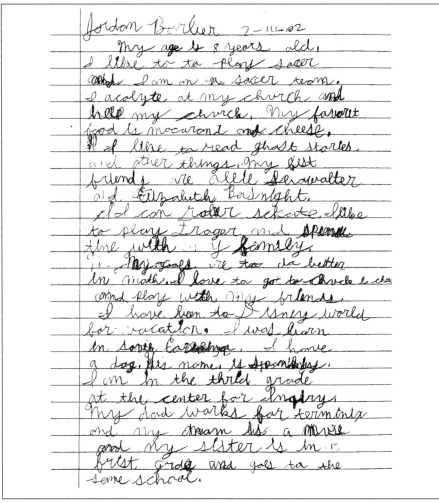

Figure 3.18. Jordan's autobiographical piece, written in February of the grade 3 school year.

Cursive was not so much an obstacle for her to overcome but a useful tool for conveying her story.

In the same reflection for the student-led conferences, Tim asked the children to read from a book of their choice and to record impressions of themselves as readers. Jordan used this reflection to prepare for demonstrating her growth for her parents at conference time (Figure 3.20).

> I noticed that I understand how to read better and I am reading longer than I used to. I used to read for 5 minutes and now I am reading for like an hour or longer.

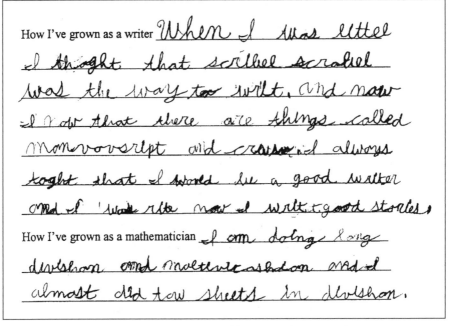

Figure 3.19. Jordan's self-evaluation of her growth as a writer.

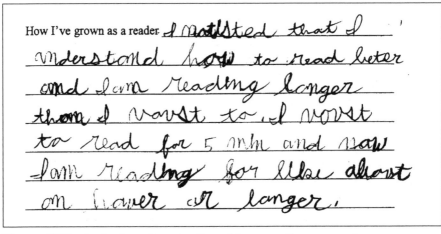

Figure 3.20. Jordan's self-evaluation of her growth as a reader.

In this short response, Jordan was able to demonstrate not only that she understood clearly the function of reading, but also that she had become a *willing* reader. She read not just because she had to but because she wanted to. This was an important milestone in Jordan's literacy development. It was not a sudden occurrence. Jordan's confidence had been building over a long period. Constant celebration of her growth as a reader and writer and a myriad opportunities to respond to reading through writing, drawing, conversation, and so forth helped her to see that she was indeed a reader.

The following story (see Figure 3.21) is out of sequence (note the lack of cursive), but we wanted to end this section with a story written by Jordan. This piece was written in response to the invitation to write a family story. Jordan chose to write about a recent family accident. This story was written toward the beginning of third grade and has been edited.

The Accident

One day my uncle was at home and he was finishing the floor with a nail gun. He pulled the trigger accidentally and tried to stop the nail but he couldn't. He shot the nail into his wrist. So he had to go to the emergency room. Meanwhile at his house, my cousin said to my aunt, "Where is daddy?" My Aunt Ren didn't want to worry her so she said, "Daddy won't be home 'til late. He has to work late and he had a meeting with his boss." At the hospital they said, "We'll have to do an x-ray on your wrist." So it took an hour to do the x-ray. They finally said, "We'll have to operate on your wrist." It took an hour to take the x-ray because it took an hour to x-ray the whole arm to make sure that the nail didn't make another bone break. He had to get a arm cast. When my Aunt Deena called him and said, "Is there anything I can do for you?" He said, "Now that you mention it, you can finish the floor." My aunt said, "Kevin, if you shot yourself, I might shoot myself." At my grandma's house, my Aunt Deena had to wake my cousin so my Aunt Ren could go and see my uncle. When my cousin was chasing my aunt's dog Taz, Taz followed my aunt into her room. My cousin said, "Why is Taz following you and not me?" My aunt said, "Because he knows me better." "No he doesn't. You only visit. I stay here." My aunt said, "Time for bed." In the night my aunt heard my cousin crying. So she called her mom and she picked her up and took her home. The End

Jordan obviously had developed a wonderful sense of story. In fact, she had always been a good storyteller, but it took some time to convince her that she could tell these stories on paper. The class always looked forward to Jordan's published pieces. In this piece, and in all of

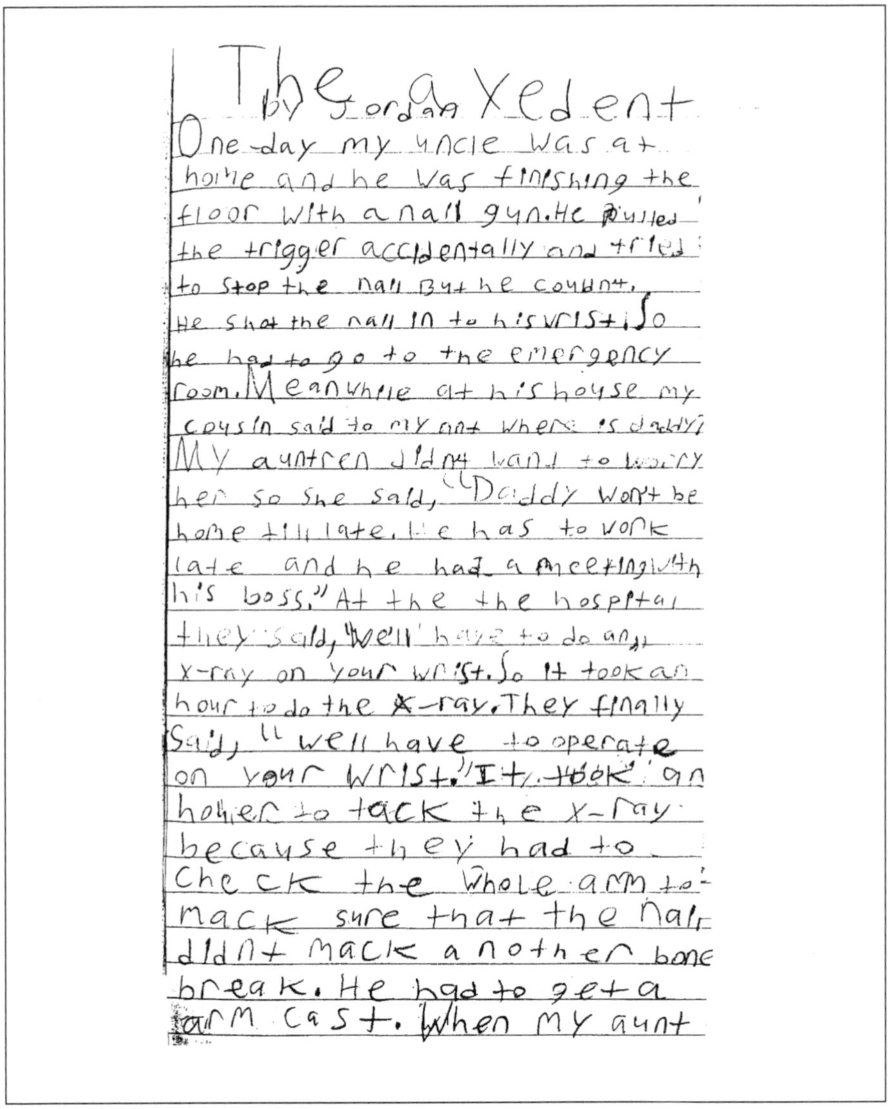

> The Xedent
> by Jordan
> One day my uncle was at home and he was finishing the floor with a nail gun. He pulled the trigger accidentally and tried to stop the nail But he couldn't. He shot the nail in to his wrist. So he had to go to the emergency room. Meanwhile at his house my cousin said to my ant where is daddy? My auntren didn't want to worry her so she said, "Daddy won't be home till late. He has to work late and he had a meeting with his boss." At the the hospital they said, "We'll have to do an x-ray on your wrist. So It took an hour to do the x-ray. They finally Said, "we'll have to operate on your wrist." It took an hour to tack the x-ray because they had to Check the whole arm to mack sure that the nail didn't mack another bone break. He had to get a arm cast. When my aunt

Figure 3.21. Jordan's family story, written around the beginning of third grade.

Jordan's workshop work, she was learning about language by taking her writing all the way through the authoring cycle. While her final draft still contained some miscues, she was able to develop her talent as a storyteller as she recorded this memorable family story. She was learning through language by using writing as a tool to communicate this event and to capture it as a record for the future. She was also learning through language about herself by documenting important aspects of her young life.

Kenan: A Gallery

The gallery of Kenan's work contains responses to some of the same invitations demonstrated in Jordan's gallery. The projects for the Halloween picture book, autobiographical responses, and reflections for student-led conferences, for example, were the same for both of these children. Kenan, however, took a different path toward literacy. Because he came to second grade already a strong reader and a conventional writer, his shifts during these two years were subtler. Although he was also learning language, learning about language, and learning through language, his was a process more of honing and refining. Kenan's main focus during this time was on learning through language as he studied the world and applied his vast curiosity to teaching himself and the class.

> Davy Crockett. I was "Davy." I was dressed. I had a hat.

In response to his first-grade teacher's request to create a class book for Halloween, Kenan wrote and drew about his character, Davy Crockett (Figure 3.22). In his drawing, Kenan has on a coonskin cap and a fringed jacket and is carrying a rubber knife in his belt. Kenan's handwriting is neat and his letters are all conventionally formed, aside from the fact that the capitals and lowercase are all the same size. He titled his paper with the name of the character he portrayed. Every word is spelled conventionally except *dressed,* which Kenan spelled *drest.* He demonstrates conventional use of capital letters except for the letter *d* and the last *h.* Perhaps this is because he began the piece with a capital *D* for Davy. It is interesting to note his use of quotation marks around *Davy.* Kenan wanted to denote Davy as a special word in this little piece. He may have thought it was appropriate to designate *Davy* as a nickname. Either way, his playful use of quotation marks reveals his willingness to experiment with more sophisticated punctuation along with periods, which he used correctly three times.

A year later, in second grade, Kenan was learning through language by contributing to the class journals. Because his parents were from Turkey, Kenan knew quite a lot of the Turkish language. Following Jordan's lead (counting to ten in Spanish), Kenan counted for the class in Turkish (see Figure 3.23). He also contributed frequently to the class science journal. In Figure 3.24, he talks about two very distinct animals from different areas on Earth.

Figure 3.22. Kenan's contribution to the first-grade Halloween class book.

Each Galapagos turtle has its own shell shape. One kick of a giraffe's hoof will crush a lion.

Kenan had been reading a book on animals and took advantage of the science journal to teach his classmates some of what he had been learning. His science journal entries were one of his most important contributions to the classroom community. He often shared his vast

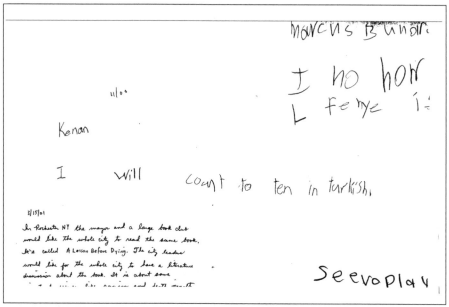

Figure 3.23. One of Kenan's language journal entries in second grade.

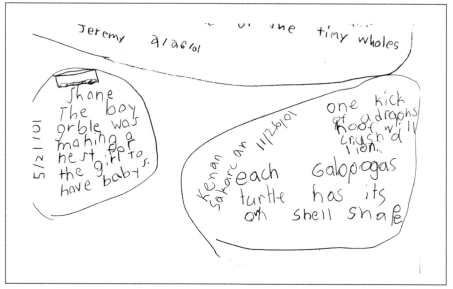

Figure 3.24. One of Kenan's science journal entries in second grade.

knowledge during morning meetings and in particular during the sharing of class journals and current events. Kenan contributed to these as much as any child in the class. He often kept the conversations alive by asking clarifying questions and adding his own bits of information to the contributions of other children.

These journal entries are somewhat unconventional looking. Written at the edge of the large journal page, Kenan's entry in Figure 3.24 is cramped. His spelling miscues indicate close attention to letter sounds. While *draphs* may not look similar to *giraffe's*, it contains many of the same sounds as Kenan's pronunciation of the word. The *ph* for the /f/ sound is an interesting miscue in that it demonstrates Kenan's experiences in reading. It is far more common for children to substitute *f* for *ph*. His spelling for *Galapagos* is close to the conventional spelling of the word and also shows a close consideration of letter sounds. Out of the eighteen words written in the entry (excluding his name), Kenan wrote sixteen words correctly (89 percent). He also erased at least once and self-corrected the word *own* by inserting a *w*. This self-monitoring indicates that he was continuing to learn about language while he was using language to learn.

When it was time for the first progress report in second grade, Tim wrote about Kenan's accomplishments as a reader and a writer. Kenan obviously had a great deal of talent, and it was one of Tim's goals for Kenan to be more productive (see Figure 3.25).

Kenan's self-evaluation accompanying the progress report is revealing in several ways (see Figure 3.26). His pluses are specific and show that he did indeed know how he had grown during the nine-week period. While the class had not studied multiplication yet per se, Kenan challenged himself with these kinds of problems and not only understood the ideas represented by these operations but was also giving himself problems to solve. The plus he gave himself in science was also very accurate. Kenan's "getting better at science and predictions" extended class discussions and clarified understandings for everyone. It is interesting that his third plus is about such a discrete language skill. Although it is true that he was continually trying to refine his writing mechanics, the quality of the content of his writing is what truly stood out to Tim and the rest of the class.

> My name is Kenan Erdem Sakarcan. I'm Turkish. My favorite food is ice cream. I like to raise plants when they are hurt. My hobby is gardening and making things out of wood. I have one sister. I collect stamps, postcards. I like swimming. I'm building a new

Center for Inquiry
Progress Report 2000–2001
Richland County School District Two & University of South Carolina *Small School Partnership*

Student:	Kenan Sakarcan
Teacher:	Tim O'Keefe
Grade:	2
Assigned to grade:	
Grading period:	XX

Child's Growth as a Reader:
Kenan is a very good reader for his age. He is confident and challenges himself with books that are difficult for many of his age mates. He has a hard time staying quiet during the time we set aside for independent reading but it is mainly because he wants so badly to share what he is reading with someone. He reads a variety of material from nonfiction books on chess and science to long chapter books by authors like Jack London (abridged, but it won't be long before he attempts the unabridged versions). When I ask him to talk to me about what he has read, he is very specific and enthusiastic in his retelling. He has a variety of strategies for tackling new or difficult words. He participates very often in our literature discussions.

Child's Growth as a Writer:
Kenan is an articulate writer. His writing is neat and conventional. He attends closely to instruction in writing. After discussing the use of quotation marks a few times, I began to see Kenan using them in his own writing. He has a strong voice as a writer. In his letter to the park naturalist at Sesqui Park he wrote, "Insect greadings (greetings) Thank you for theaching me how to catch insecst the right way I chahgt 4 bugs with a good partner." I do think that Kenan could push himself to be more productive.

Child's Growth as a Learner in General:
Kenan is a great kid. He comes into class each day full of enthusiasm. He is an important part of the personality of this class. He is very curious and asks wonderful questions. In this way, he is a good example for the rest of the children. He obviously enjoys learning new things. When we are on a topic that interests him, Kenan pays close attention to conversations and instruction. Other times it is difficult to get him to attend. He is taking responsibility for his own actions more and more. He is sincere about being sorry for his mistakes. At the same time, he exhibits the kind of compassion for others who are less fortunate. That is wonderful for a child. I am very proud that he is taking responsibility for the UNICEF project. He is helpful around the classroom and helpful to his friends when he can be. He has a great sense of humor and is fun to be around. I am very glad that he is in our class.

Figure 3.25. Tim's first second-grade narrative progress report for Kenan.

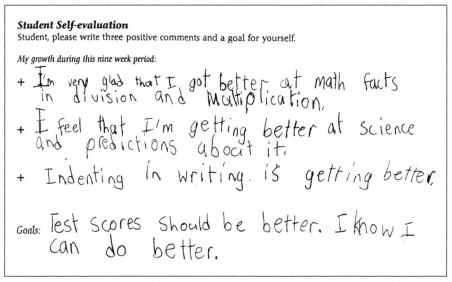

Student Self-evaluation
Student, please write three positive comments and a goal for yourself.

My growth during this nine week period:

+ I'm very glad that I got better at math facts in division and Multiplication.

+ I feel that I'm getting better at science and predictions about it.

+ Indenting in writing is getting better.

Goals: Test scores should be better. I know I can do better.

Figure 3.26. Kenan's self-evaluation at the end of the first nine weeks of second grade.

house in Wildwood. My dad is a engineer. My favorite sport is soccer. My favorite animal is the killer whale. The food I like least is okra. My favorite board game is chess. I used to collect Digimon and Pokemon cards. My favorite book series are the Hardy Boys. I also like Nancy Drew.

In August, Kenan created his short autobiographical piece (Figures 3.27 and 3.28). In about fifteen minutes, he wrote about his Turkish background, hobbies, family, and likes and dislikes. His writing for this piece was factual and, like that of many of his peers, similar to a list. It is a time capsule of his life at the beginning of third grade. His writing here is very conventional. Although this piece hung on the wall among the other autobiographical sketches, Kenan continued to read it and to edit it. At one point, he went over to the bulletin board display of autobiographies and inserted the word *to* in the fifth line to make that sentence grammatically correct. He also added the last two sentences about his favorite book series while the paper hung on the wall. Kenan's attention to detail and his willingness to revise his piece even as it hung on the bulletin board demonstrated his commitment to learning about language. Reworking his piece, however slightly, confirmed his work ethic and his high level of investment. This set him apart from many other students.

Figure 3.27. Kenan's self-portrait at the beginning of third grade.

On September 11, 2001, Tim heard the news about the terrorist bombings in New York and Washington, D.C., from his principal while the children were on the recess field. The staff decided to let the parents tell the children what had happened in their own ways. When the children came into the room the next morning, all of them wanted to talk about the news. For morning work, Tim asked everyone to write down whatever they wanted to share about the news and to bring it to morning meeting. Some children drew pictures of the fiery crash of the planes into the World Trade Center. Stephanie wrote, "It is so sad that I think I am going to cry." Jordan wrote, "I feel so sorry for the children who don't have mommies and daddies now." Margaret wrote, "A very tall building that just crumbled. They think about a million people died." Paxie wrote, "They might start another war. . . It is sad for me. A lot of people died in this because of the building collapsing. It hurts bad inside because of this." Other written comments included: "I think it was a tragic loss to America," "Maybe something went wrong with the plane or something," and Amber's "My heart is with all those families that are lost. I also know that God is with me and will help us get through this." Kenan wrote (see Figure 3.29):

> A building got rammed into by a plane. They suspect a terrorism group. Some people say we're going to war.

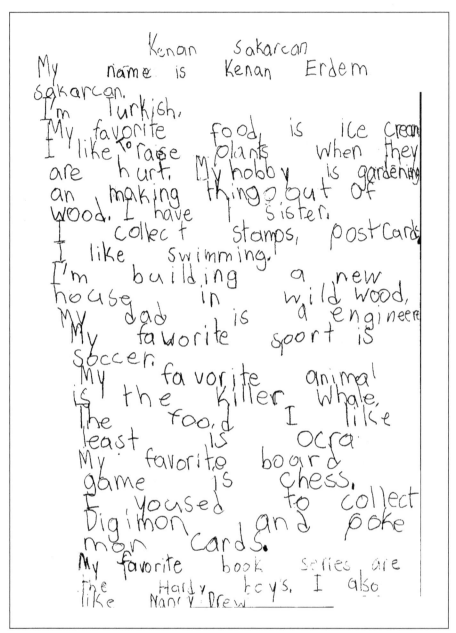

Figure 3.28. Kenan's autobiographical piece written at the beginning of third grade.

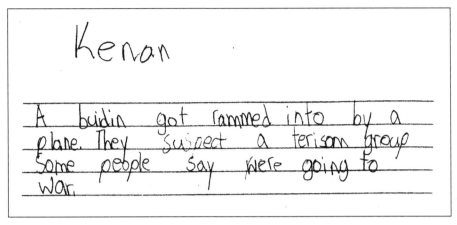

Kenan

A buidin got rammed into by a plane. They suspect a terison group Some people say were going to war.

Figure 3.29. Kenan's written response to the 9/11 terrorist attacks.

When the conversation began, Kenan was unusually quiet. Many children read what they had written, and a somber attitude pervaded the room. Tim let the children say whatever they wanted before making any comment of his own. He saw it as his job to make sure the children felt safe and that any misinterpretations of the news were cleared up. The children sat in a circle. Each child, in turn, read or just talked about his or her impressions of the news. Kenan was seated on the floor next to Tim and was the last child to speak before Tim opened up the discussion to everyone.

Tim was in awe of Kenan's knowledge and sympathy as he took his turn speaking. First, Kenan dispelled the idea that there was going to be a war in South Carolina. "You don't have to be scared," he said. "No one's going to hurt us here." He cleared up much of the confusion and laid many fears to rest. One child, a good friend of Kenan's, had said earlier that the terrorists were Muslim and that they were essentially "the bad guys." Kenan is Muslim and the remark hurt him badly. For the few minutes that Kenan spoke, the class was totally quiet. The idea he conveyed was that while the terrorists may have been Muslim, most Muslims are good people. With tears in his eyes, he asked that the class remember their studies of civil rights and black history. He asked everyone to remember not to judge people by the color of their skin or their religion but by their character and actions. No one could have said it more clearly. When Kenan was finished, Tim had little to say. Kenan had said in very few words what most people could not have said in hours.

This story is not included to represent any significant sign of reading or writing growth on Kenan's part but rather to demonstrate his character. Kenan was not a perfect student in every way. He was so competitive, for example, that soccer at recess had to be cancelled because of the arguments that often surrounded Kenan and a few others. But Kenan had a rare, quiet sincerity that was truly inspiring at times. This was one of those times.

Kenan loved to read. In his reading logs, he often recorded two hours or more of reading each night. He was also adept at responding to literature in meaningful ways. For literature study after the winter holiday, the class read *Owl Moon* by Jane Yolen (1977). In this quiet story, a child accompanies her father on a nighttime walk in the cold winter woods searching for owls. Finally, after much perseverance, the two call down an owl that flies over them in the night. Kenan's first sentence in his literature response was "I think the most important thing you take when you go owling is patience." This is a classic example of Kenan taking an ordinary assignment and writing an extraordinary response. Kenan skipped past comprehension issues and went straight to a metaphorical response. Later, in a written conversation with his mother about the same story, Kenan said that he would call the story *Night of the Owl* rather than *Owl Moon* because the moon is merely mentioned in the story.

In January, the third graders got together for the first of several literature study interactions with their fifth grade "book buddies." The children read "The Birds' Peace" by Jean Craighead George in *The Big Book for Peace* (Durell & Sachs, 1990). The children took turns reading the story about a girl named Kristy whose father goes off to an unnamed war. Kristy runs crying into a forest clearing and recognizes a little bird there she has named Fluter. Kristy speaks of her fears for her father who "doesn't even know how to shoot a gun." Suddenly Fluter and his mate feel threatened by a strange bird invading their territory. The birds mark their territories by singing "an invisible fence of sound" and flying around their sections of the meadow. The birds find peace as Kristy writes to her father, "I know how the birds keep the peace."

Kenan and his fifth-grade book buddy, Scott, had a lengthy written conversation about this story (Figure 3.30):

> *Kenan:* How do you think the birds keep the peace?
>
> *Scott:* Probably by making their own territory and then filling it with peaceful song. What else do you think she wrote on the letter?

Figure 3.30. Kenan and Scott's written conversation about "The Birds' Peace."

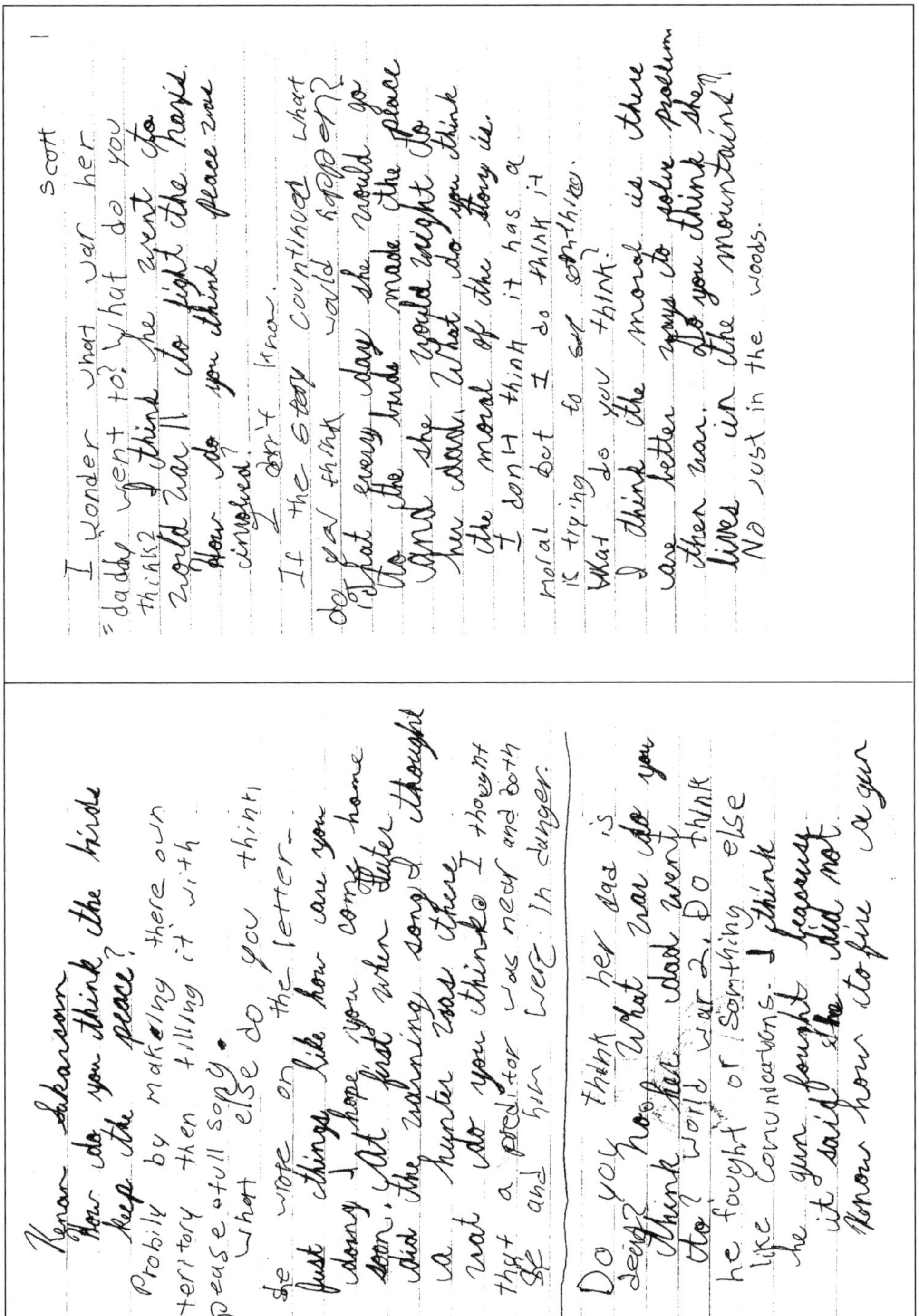

Scott

I wonder what war her
"daddy went to? What do you
think? I think he went to
World War II to fight the hard.
How do you think peace was
evolved?
— I don't know.
If the story continued what
do you think would happen?
I think every day she could go
to the birds made the peace
And she would might go
her dad. What do you think
the moral of the story is.
I don't think it has a
moral but I do think it
is trying to tel something.
What do you think.
I think the moral is there
are better ways to solve problem
then war. If you think then
lives in the mountains
No just in the woods.

Kenan Shawano
How do you think the birds
keep the peace?
Probily by making there own
territory then killing it with
peace + full song.
What else do you think,

He wrote on the letter—
Just things like how are you
doing. I hope you come home
soon. At first when hunter
did they warning song I thought
a hunter was there
wat do you think? I thought
that a preditor was near and both
he and him wer in danger.

Do you think her dad is
dead? No. What war do you
think that dad went
to. World war 2. Do think
he fought or something else
like communcations. I think
he gun fought because
it said the did not
know how to fire a gun

Kenan: Just things like how are you doing, I hope you can come home soon. At first when Fluter did the warning song, I thought a hunter was there. What did you think?

Scott: I thought that a predator was near and both she and him were in danger. Do you think her dad is dead?

Kenan: No. What war do you think her dad went to?

Scott: World War 2. Do you think he fought or something else like communications?

Kenan: I think he gun fought because it said he did not know how to fire a gun.

Scott: I wonder what war her "daddy" went to? What do you think?

Kenan: I think he went to World War II to fight the Nazis. How do you think peace was involved?

Scott: I don't know. If the story continued, what do you think would happen?

Kenan: That every day she would go to [where] the birds made the peace and she would write to her dad. What do you think the moral of the story is?

Scott: I don't think it has a moral but I do think it is trying to say something. What do you think?

Kenan: I think the moral is there are better ways to solve problems than war. Do you think she lives in the mountains?

Scott: No, just in the woods.

These written conversations were the warm-up for a larger, whole-group conversation about the story, but Kenan and Scott took hold of this opportunity and made the most of it. Their conversation demonstrates an obvious commitment to encouraging each other to think deeply about the story. Both boys assumed comprehension and pushed the other toward detailed interpretation. Kenan began by seeking Scott's ideas about the big question, "How do you think the birds keep the peace?" Scott's thoughtful response about the birds' filling their territories "with peaceful song" makes it clear right from the start that both boys are seeking to learn through language. They make a sincere attempt to know what the other knows, to gain an understanding of the other's insights.

In this interaction, neither boy asks a recall question, which are so common among the questions asked after the stories in many basal textbooks. So many of their questions contain the words *"What do you think?"* Kenan gives his initial guess about Fluter's warning song, the possibility that it might have been a hunter, and then asks Scott for his early prediction with the words *"What do you think?"* Scott replies with an equally plausible prediction, "that a predator was near."

Later, Scott wonders to himself what war her "daddy" was in and follows his inquiry with *"What do you think?"* A few sentences later Kenan asks about Scott's interpretation of the moral. Scott turns the question right back to Kenan with *"What do you think?"* Kenan reveals his own insight about war not being the best way to solve conflicts.

In this piece, Kenan reveals so much about himself as a writer and a thinker. In terms of conventions, Kenan was a competent, confident writer. His newly learned cursive writing was neat and, while it did not entirely match the model on the wall in his classroom, it is easy to read here. He made very few miscues with spelling, capitalization, and punctuation, and none of them detracted from the conversation. Kenan did omit a question mark at the end of his second question and a period in his next response. Scott good-naturedly corrected him by putting periods in both places and circling them. This is yet another example of Kenan learning about language (his slight miscues with punctuation) while learning through language. Both boys grew as critical thinkers and language users through this interaction.

The final story in Kenan's gallery of work is a lengthy piece from writing workshop from the fall of his third-grade year (Figures 3.31 and 3.32). Kenan was inspired by a picture from Tim's picture file of five dogs sitting side by side on a bench. The dogs are all large but clearly different breeds: a husky, a German shepherd, a Dalmatian, a black Labrador retriever, and a bluetick hound. This might not be the most sophisticated piece Kenan wrote while he was in Tim's class, but it demonstrates his creative spirit and his well-developed sense of story. It also shows his sense of humor and captures, in some small way, his sense of adventure.

Puppy Run by Kenan Sakarcan

The Great Escape

Chapter One: Close Call
One puppy named Kasey was scampering around a dump looking for food. When he spotted a gang of nasty looking dogs, and they looked hungry. He ran and hid but it made a big noise. "Hey, boss, what's that?" said a Chinese pug. "Don't know but it sounds like lunch," said the boss nastily.

Chapter Two: Rescued
Kasey hoped the boss would not find him. Kasey was hiding neatly under an old apartment's staircase. The boss was coming

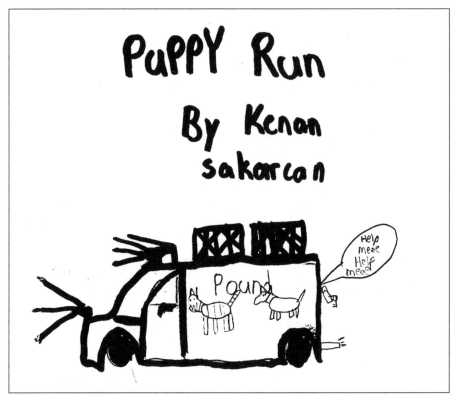

Figure 3.31. Title page of a story Kenan wrote in the fall of third grade.

right at him. Then someone's mouth picked him up. When he saw his rescuer, Kasey was shocked. It was the German shepherd, Wiley his old friend who had survived World War II.

Chapter Three: Meet the Gang
Wiley said, "If you want to stay with me you can." When they arrived, Kasey saw that he definitely wanted to stay. Casey met all the other dogs. Their names were Speed, Sherlock, Hunt, and Spots.

Chapter Four: Missing
Early in the morning Speed went to give Kasey breakfast but he was gone. Speed rushed to Wiley and said, "The kid is gone!" Wiley sniffed. "He's at the pound!" exclaimed Wiley.

Chapter Five: On the Trail
"Speed, go catch up with the pound truck," said Wiley. We'll take the shortcut. We'll meet at Reggie's Alley. They finally met at Reggie's Alley. They made camp. The next morning Wiley said, "The pound is five miles from here. We're going to get him today."

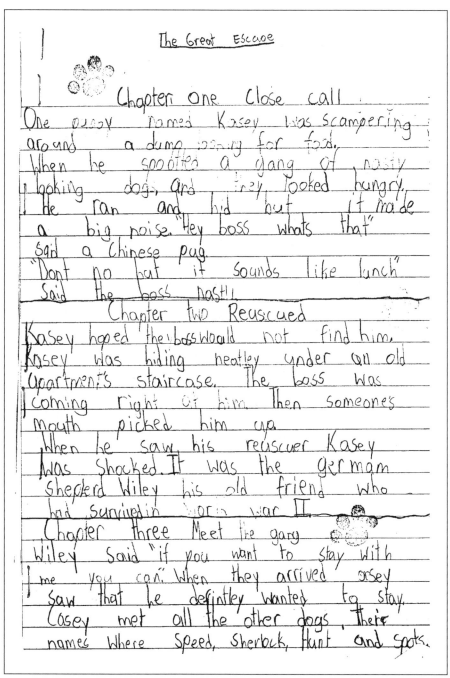

The Great Escaoe

Chapter One Close call

One puppy named Kasey was scampering around a dump searcy for food. When he spooiled a gang of nasty looking dogs and they looked hungry. He ran and hid but it made a big noise. "Hey boss whats that" said a Chinese pug. "Dont no but it sounds like lunch" said the boss nastly.

Chapter two Reuscued

Kasey hoped the boss would not find him. Kasey was hiding neatley under an old apartment's staircase. The boss was coming right at him. Then someone's mouth picked him up. When he saw his reuscuer Kasey was shocked. It was the germam shepterd Wiley his old friend who had survived in world war II.

Chapter three Meet the garg

Wiley said "if you want to stay with me you can." When they arrived orsey saw that he defintley wanted to stay. Casey met all the other dogs. Their names where Speed, Sherbck, Hunt and spots.

Figure 3.32. The first chapters of Kenan's two-titled story *Puppy Run/The Great Escape.*

Chapter Six: The Great Escape
Then they arrived at the pound. They heard a voice say, "Hey, guys! Over here!" "There he is," exclaimed Sherlock. "Speed, you stay lookout," said Hunt. Then Wiley said, "Spots, help me open the gate." "Someone's coming," said Speed. "Try again," said Wiley. "Got it," said Spots. Then the alarm went wooo, woooo, woooo. "Dogs on the loose," said a pound worker. Hunt pulled out a net and threw it on him. Speed pushed a bag of dog food and conked one on the head. Several other dogcatchers went for Wiley but he pushed two barrels of dog food and knocked the dogcatchers out.

The End

On the Value of Writing to Learn

It is only fitting to close this chapter with another story, a story that reveals the importance of writing to learn. Kenan and Jordan are in fourth grade now. Last week we saw Jordan on the playground. We mentioned that it seemed as though we were still living and learning with her because we have been thinking so much about her through the writing of this chapter. She responded without skipping a beat, "Yeah, I understand what you mean. It's like when I did my genealogy project on my grandpa in first grade. When I was looking at his pictures all the time and telling stories about him and writing about him, it was like he was still alive with me. He really isn't, but doing that project kind of brought him back to life for me." And so it is with us as teachers. The more we think, talk, and write about our students, the more we understand them and truly bring them to life.

4 Literacy, Inquiry, and Democratic Practices

The mission of the Center for Inquiry describes a particular kind of learning community:

"The parents, students, and staff of the Center for Inquiry . . . are responsible for developing ourselves as more thoughtful, caring, and intelligent people who delight in learning and are committed to creating a more compassionate, equitable, knowledgeable, and democratic world."

In this chapter, we look closely at the ways in which inquiry and literacy can help children grow as thoughtful, caring actors who contribute to, in Dewey's (1938/1963) words, a "democratic way of life."

The word *democracy* conjures up a range of definitions and views. Our view is closely related to Beyer's (1996) vision of a "revitalized" democracy. In this vision, citizens are actively involved in the decisions and negotiations that affect their lives and community. Such participation means that all community members contribute, beyond the ballot box, to making their community a better place. An emerging body of work describes what such democratizing practices look like in classrooms and schools. This work describes ways in which students are actively engaged in classroom life through many opportunities to develop the skills and understandings necessary to be active participants in their classrooms and in their communities. Some of this work goes further, underscoring how children can look at their world with an eye for justice and learn to contribute in ways that lead to an even more democratic, equitable, caring society (Allen, 1999; Beane & Apple, 1995; Becker & Couto, 1996; Edelsky, 1994; Freire, 1970/1995, 1973/1998; Goodman, 1992; Greene, 1988, 1995; Jennings & Green, 1999; Shor, 1992; Yeager, Pattenaude, Franquiz, & Jennings, 1999). These are the kinds of goals and practices we think about when we refer to democratic ways of life in classrooms.

Not surprisingly, we see talk as being at the heart of such a democratic life. Through language, literacy, and inquiry, Tim fosters democratic practices that are both caring and critical. In his classroom, essential elements of a democratic way of life include community building, deliberation, thoughtful participation, compassion, caring, and equity. The following vignette demonstrates these qualities:

Knowing they would be together the following year, Tim proposed to his second graders a summer teaching-learning project: During the summer, each member of the class, including Tim, would prepare a "lesson" about a topic or skill of their choice, such as the topic of optical lenses or the skill of macramé. Then, during the first weeks of school, each person would teach his or her lesson to the rest of the class. The next year Tim asked the students to observe qualities of good teaching while they were engaged in the projects. When all projects were complete, they gathered on the carpet to discuss what they had learned about teaching and learning. Tim started the conversation:

"Think of the different projects and what we learned from them. You can talk about something that didn't work well without being negative. You can turn it around and put it in a positive way. For example, instead of saying 'don't mumble,' you can say 'it's important to speak clearly when you are teaching.'" Tim wrote the children's ideas on chart paper as they offered them, under the headings "good teacher" and "good student." When one child offered several ideas in a row, Tim suggested they take turns by raising their hands.

Jack suggested that a quality of a good student was being interested and paying attention. Lora added that good teachers offer interesting topics.

Jack noticed that being appreciative was in the student column but should also be in the teacher column because good teachers appreciate their students' ideas. Sarah added that appreciative teachers show respect for their students, and students are being respectful when they appreciate the teacher's efforts and knowledge.

Dani extended Jack's and Sarah's ideas by noting that the teacher should also pay attention to the students when they are talking or asking a question.

Lora raised her hand again and suggested, "Teachers should teach in an interesting way."

Tim responded, "That seems to be the crux of it all. Can you say more about that?"

Lora thought about it, and then said that teachers need to be interesting, and another student said it was important to be enthusiastic. Tim offered an example of a friend who took a video course on astronomy but found it boring because the class was just told to read and listen. He added, "Many of you did hands-on teaching and learning, and it was great. You really got us involved in what you were teaching. Like Lora said, you were teaching in an interesting way."

The class continued to discuss the merits of good students when the conversation worked back to teaching. Tim noted that it was important that Elise didn't talk down to them when she was teaching. A student asked Tim to explain what he meant. "Some teachers won't use certain words because they see that as grown-up language. But adults can talk to kids like they talk to each other."

Cameron wrapped up the conversation: "It seems like it's important to have a goal to teach and be willing to work hard to achieve the goals."

Tim reviewed aloud the list and said with a smile, "That's a great list; it would be hard for adults to generate such a rich list of qualities of teachers and learners." He and the children talked about how this chart could guide them through the year as they taught and learned together, serving as a form of "charter" of classroom rights and responsibilities. In fact, Tim described the activity and posted this chart in the next weekly newsletter to parents.

This vignette showcases many important qualities of a democratic way of classroom life and the role of language in this process. First, there was thoughtful participation—everyone took on the roles of both teacher and learner as they offered ideas and responded to them. By asking students to take turns, Tim encouraged equitable participation. The class used language that honored their compassion for one another by critiquing the projects in constructive ways. As inquirers, they carefully observed and attended to one another, posing questions, extending ideas, and making connections as they deliberated about the qualities they wanted in their class community. Tim validated and clarified their ideas by committing them to paper, which was posted as a class charter of rights and responsibilities. Conversations and writing activities like these give children opportunities to learn, learn about, and learn through language that is essential to democratic deliberation and participation. It is worth taking a closer look at the role of language and inquiry in fostering the democratic way of life that is evident in the school's mission statement:

- Building community through thoughtful deliberation and participation
- Compassion and caring
- Equity and diversity

Building Community through Thoughtful Deliberation and Participation. A recent buzzword in education is *community building.* Tim's classroom community is not solely a place where all people get along, although it is a peaceful classroom. As evident from the previous chapters and the vignette above, Tim and his students form a certain kind of community—a community of caring, thoughtful inquirers. As they interact, talk, and share their diverse perspectives, Tim and his students often negotiate how they will live and work together. In this way, children learn how to deliberate and make decisions together. The vignette demonstrates how each member of the class had a part to play in exploring how they would teach and learn together that year. In Tim's classroom, everybody has responsibility for contributing to the community, and all voices are respected, even when all voices aren't in agreement. As children participate and contribute actively and thoughtfully to the class community, they play a part in developing and transforming it (Gutmann, 1999; Jennings & Green, 1999; Jennings, O'Keefe, & Shamlin, 1999; Wolk, 1998). Through class conversations such as this one, Tim's students have the opportunity to practice thinking critically, communicating effectively, and actively making a difference in their classroom community.

Compassion and Caring. Throughout the day, Tim emphasizes that they all need to be respectful of and thoughtful toward one another as they share their insights and wonders. Compassion is important in a democracy, for it is compassion that helps us be aware of others in our community and see the value of contributing to the common good. In other words, democratic communities are caring places (Jennings, 2000; Noddings, 1984). Sometimes during morning meetings, for example, everybody takes a turn complimenting another person in the class. But it is also important that the students practice respect and caring outside of these explicit opportunities to recognize one another. Tim helps children learn language and use language that fosters a caring community. As the children share their questions, ideas, and opinions across the curriculum, they learn how to respond to one another with appreciation and to disagree with respect, as Judith Lindfors

(1999) illustrated so well in Karen Gallas's and Karen Smith's classrooms.

Diversity and Equity. All classrooms are diverse, for each person sees the world differently according to her or his gender, ethnic background, family life, learning experiences, and other cultural factors. Tim and the children make sense of the world by teaching and learning with and from one another, striving to give equal weight to all these diverse voices. By sharing the various ways in which they learn and understand, people have an opportunity to learn from one another, thus providing equitable access to knowledge. By sharing strategies for solving a math problem or reading a sentence, for example, children gain access to one another's knowledge and perspectives. They begin to see that there is often no one "right" solution, but rather a variety of angles and possibilities to consider. All inquiry is an act of simultaneous teaching and learning (Lindfors, 1999; Mills, 2001). Tim and the children develop classroom rituals that help the children learn and use language in ways that honor diversity and equity.

We can't assume that children come to school with all the language, social skills, attitudes, and understandings needed to create a smooth-working, democratic class community. In fact, adults often struggle with such pursuits themselves. This chapter illustrates how Tim creates literacy and inquiry practices, that help students learn how to take an active part in democratic life. As we illustrate, through these literacy and inquiry practices, the class was largely learning about democracy through language and learning language that helped them to develop these democratic ways of classroom life by:

- building knowledge together
- acting with caring and compassion
- learning to critique
- contributing to the class community

Building Knowledge Together

The premise behind learning in Tim's classroom is that all members of the class share and build on one another's knowledge. As seen in Chapter 2, this occurs in many ways. The class discusses observations and questions raised in the class journals, for example, and they discuss news items brought in by the students or Tim. Throughout these discussions, they connect knowledge they already have to new information. They use language to inquire together. Now we consider how such knowledge sharing is a democratic process.

In the beginning of second grade, Tim and the students engage in an activity they call WDYKATN?—"What Do You Know About This Number?" On the first day of school, they'll talk about what they know about the number one. On day 5, here is what some of the discussion sounded like:

Victoria: My sister is five years old and she's in kindergarten.

Tim: What's her name?

Victoria: Margaret.

Tim: Okay, she's five. Lora?

Lora: It's easy to, um, to do math with.

Tim: Okay, can you give us an example?

Lora: Like counting by fives.

Tim: Yes, for some reason it seems easier to count by fives. Why do you think that is?

Lora: Because you already know it.

Faith: You have five fingers on your hands.

Tim: Yes, and you know, I think that's really important and goes with what Lora said.

Thomas: Five plus five equals ten so you've got, you've got ten fingers.

Tim: So I'm guessing that the five fingers on one hand is part of the reason that we count by fives so much, because we have it so ready. You know, five, ten, fifteen, twenty, like that. Here's one thing I know about the number five—its cool number patterns. Count by fives with me so that I can write it down. Ready?

Students: 5, 10, 15, 20, 25, 30, 35, 40, 45, 50 [Tim lists the numbers on the board].

Tim: All right. Does anyone notice any patterns when you're looking at this?

Elaina: Um, well, if you go down the row, you are always gonna see five on one side, five then zero, then five then zero.

Tim: All right, so if you look in the ones place—this [pointing] is called the ones place—did you guys talk about that in first grade?

Students: Yeah, yes.

Tim: The ones place is 5, 0, 5, 0, 5, 0, so that's a great pattern there. So that's one reason it's easy to count by fives.

The conversation continued for several more minutes about patterns in the tens place, thermometers and clocks marked in fives, that people have five senses, and that most people have five toes. Throughout the discussion, students were bringing in their knowledge about the number five and using that knowledge as a basis for further inquiry and exploration. The students' and the teacher's personal knowledge was valued and could be connected to more formal school knowledge. The fact that Victoria's sister was five years old was a useful context for these young children, giving them a sense of what the number five can mean. Lora's recognition that it's easier to do math with fives led to a rich exploration of number patterns and how such patterns function in mathematics. Tim could have started with that information and presented it to the students rather than building from students' knowledge and insights. By building from students' language and knowledge, though, the children gain a sense that their ideas and knowledge matter and are worth voicing. This is important for developing skills of democratic deliberation. The students are learning mathematics through language as well as learning how to build knowledge together by sharing and extending what they already know.

From Tim's perspective, these open-ended discussions help to uncover so much more in a given content area than he would have been able to offer alone. The children come to understand very quickly that it is their right, and even their responsibility, to help fill in the gaps. This practice isn't meant just to help children think they are involved in creating curriculum—they understand that they are an essential part of everyday life and instruction in the class. So structures such as WDYKATN?, class journals, news, strategy sharing, and literature discussions place at the center of the curriculum the knowledge and language of the children, and this knowledge and language can then be expanded.

In democratic classrooms, the student and teacher roles are often taken up by both children and adults. Tim often participates as a learner, gaining new information and perspectives from the children, and the children often become the teacher. In third grade, for example, Victoria shared news from an astronomy magazine that she and her father liked to read together:

> *Victoria:* I got an article in a magazine and it's about Neptune
> and Uranus. They were experimenting with gases, they
> made gases from Neptune and there's a lot of pressure
> there. And when they pushed it together, the gases, then it
> made crystals, so they're thinking that it rains crystals on

Neptune and Uranus. They're thinking that Neptune has a big diamond in the middle of it. About the size of Earth.

Cameron: A diamond the size of Earth?

Tim: You know what diamonds are made out of? A very common element on Earth—carbon.

Victoria: Uh huh. And they have a lot of carbon there and they have a lot of pressure, and so when they push it together, it makes the crystal, and so they're thinking that there's a whole bunch of crystals on Neptune and Uranus.

Ryan: If there's a big diamond on Uranus, I bet they have littler diamonds on the surface.

Victoria: Yeah, it like rains, like our rain is like their diamonds. But they're not really sure. But they're thinking that.

Faith: Maybe, if that's really true, Victoria, maybe the people . . . like since people have gone to certain planets and the moon and stuff, maybe they'll go to Uranus and try and see if it's true, but nobody will probably get there and still be alive when they come back.

Victoria: Neptune is the one that they're pretty sure has the big diamond in the middle of it. But they're not as positive, they don't think it as much for Uranus, but they think that more about Neptune. But they're not that sure.

Victoria's passion for astronomy comes through clearly in this vignette. She masterfully summarized a fairly complex scientific news story for the class and responded to students' comments about the story. She was careful to point out that this is a hypothesis based on knowledge scientists already have, but that further study is needed before a firm conclusion can be reached. Tim played a small role in clarifying Victoria's summary by adding information about carbon. Victoria picked up the discussion from there very handily. The other children naturally interacted with Victoria in exploring this topic, as they addressed their comments and questions to her, even using her name. Not only were the children learning about astronomy through language, but they were also learning how to share and build on one another's knowledge. And they did so with compassion and care, other qualities critical to democratic class communities.

Acting with Compassion and Caring

Christine arrived in third grade quiet and shy. Tim discovered that she enjoyed playing chess, and they began playing together each morning. Other students grew interested, so Christine and Tim taught them chess rules. Soon many children could be found playing chess each morning, discussing strategies with one another. They decided to have a friendly class chess tournament. Then the second grade invited the third graders to teach them how to play chess. The following vignette illustrates the compassion and caring evident in these chess scenarios.

> In one morning meeting during third grade, Tim observed that people were exhibiting good sportsmanship during their class chess tournament.
> "Everybody figured out a way to fix their problems," he commended.
> When a student mentioned that they would be teaching chess to the second-grade class, Tim asked for their ideas about organizing this event. The children talked about ways they could be good teachers, such as exercising patience, giving gentle reminders, and going over the basics before playing a game. Lora then suggested that they use a random cup in order to match up third-grade chess teachers with second-grade chess learners, a practice they used for matching up book buddies with another class.
> Tim responded, "Cool, we could have chess buddies!"
> Lora added, "And then, like, every other week we could get together and play a chess tournament."
> They then all discussed how they could make sure they had enough chess boards for both classes by sharing their class boards and bringing in loaners from home.

This vignette illustrates a practice of language that emphasizes community, compassion, and caring. First, Tim explicitly brought up the topic of sportsmanship and commended the students for interacting fairly and respectfully during their class chess tournament. He invited them to share their ideas for organizing chess instruction with another class, rather than arranging this solely with the other teacher. So as a community, they brainstormed ways of teaching chess to other kids and equitable ways of organizing Lora's idea of chess buddies. They talked about how to be compassionate teachers of chess, teachers who are constructive and patient with learners. They also talked about how they could share their resources with the other class, another sign of a caring community. Compassion and caring are an important part of this school and Tim's class, and these qualities are woven into the academic day in many ways (Jennings, 2000; O'Keefe, 2001). Tim uses additional rituals and strategies for developing a community of caring children.

One of the morning meeting rituals the students suggested in second grade was a continuation of a ritual they had had in first grade with Michele Shamlin: sharing compliments. By going around the circle and voicing commendable things they had noticed about one another, they became attuned to observing and articulating one another's attributes as learners and as people. Dani, for example, thanked Taylor for helping her with a math problem; Michael appreciated the class for being good listeners when he presented his expert project; and Elaina remarked that she had noticed that Faith was working hard on her handwriting and doing a beautiful job of developing her writing.

Louise noticed that over the years the children grew more sophisticated in what they observed and found noteworthy about one another, and that this activity helped them develop more compassion toward one another as learners. Because this was a new skill for many of them in kindergarten, Michele made suggestions about what they might notice about one another throughout the day and how they could voice these observations. This ritual became a worthwhile part of the academic day and played a critical role in community building. Children pointed out, for example, successful features of a student's story that was published by being read aloud during writing workshop. The students valued this ritual and asked Tim if they could continue it in second grade. Tim agreed. With time this practice became integrated into the community in less formal ways. By then, it seems, it had become natural to take careful note of one another and respond with compassion and care. We think of this behavior as "response-ability." Nell Noddings (1984) discusses how compassion begins with noticing other people and responding to them—their needs, their views, their actions. It means being aware that you are an individual within a community of others, and being aware of your role in maintaining the common good of this community.

Tim also uses music in many rituals that emphasize compassion and caring. Music is one of Tim's loves, and in many ways it serves as a kind of glue in his class. Each class community develops its own brand of adhesive. When Louise taught middle school social studies, maps and cultures were the glue. Heidi has always tied her classrooms together through children's literature. In Tim's room, one of the class jobs is the music person, whose responsibility includes turning on a musical tape to signal the start of morning meeting. This is a gentle way to gather and begin the day together. The cleanup song, which changes as children make suggestions of new songs, allows children three to four minutes to finish conversations, put away games, or shelve their books. Tim's love for music makes this a natural method for signaling that it's time to gather; other teachers use chimes, poems, or other unobtrusive sounds or sights. These signals keep the teacher from having to raise her or his voice to corral students. This subtle and simple tool helps set the tone for a caring, compassionate class community.

Tim usually concludes the morning meeting by leading the class in song. He plays guitar and sometimes the children accompany him with percussion instruments. This is a joyful shared experience. The songs, all written on chart paper, range from traditional children's melodies, to classic songs such as "Old Susannah," to folk songs, to rock, to school favorites, to songs authored by the class or prior classes. Tim also likes connecting the kids to previous generations through "older" songs, such as "Country Road" by John Denver. Also, groups of children will work with Tim to create songs, and sometimes the entire class writes lyrics to a tune. These songs usually relate to something they are studying, such as the planets or countries. This is another way these learners develop and use language that allows them to build a strong class community.

Learning to Critique and Express Opinions

We've described how democracy is practiced and fostered through literacy and inquiry activities as the kids and teachers talk and interact. But it's also important to learn about community and democracy by explicitly studying, talking about, and critiquing democratic principles. This section focuses on ways that children learn language to articulate their views as citizens and learn *about* democracy *through* language. Particularly, we focus on Egawa and Harste's (2001) notion of learning to use language to critique. When we speak of critique, we mean teaching children to "read" their social worlds and "read between the lines" to uncover how people's actions create just and unjust practices in our society (Banks, 1995; Freire, 1970/1995). Many educators believe that children in primary grades are too young for such conversations. But we have seen how children wonder about social issues and seek to find ways to understand and talk about them. And this process is congruent with social studies standards that focus on critically analyzing texts and the world. Tim has explored many avenues for supporting young children in these efforts.

Throughout each school year, Tim and the children discuss a wide range of social texts: newspaper articles, letters to the editor, and results of polls. They also read and talk about books and stories written for children about the civil rights movement, human rights, and war and peace (Jennings, 2002). This section of the chapter focuses on class discussions about social issues in the students' local community and the world.

Interpreting Graphic Texts

In a democratic society, active, informed citizens need to be able to interpret opinion polls, surveys, graphs, and the use of statistics. Tim often shares with students such graphics about local, national, and international issues. One day, for example, he shared graphs from the local newspaper that reflected statewide voting patterns. The class studied the graphs and discussed how the poll was a sampling of citizens. They also talked about how the pollsters used mathematical methods to get a sample that represented the larger population.

One day in third grade, Tim announced that each student would start receiving a copy of *Time* magazine for children. He shared an article from one issue about the increasing rate of growth of the world population. The following vignette illustrates how children were using language to critically read the graph.

Tim started the conversation by saying, "Remember how earlier we talked about the world population reaching 6 billion? It says here that everybody on the planet needs food, water, and fuel. These resources are limited, and everyone will need to use them sparingly so there's enough for the next 6 billion people added to our world. Here's a really nice graph; it's similar to the one in the Sunday paper."

As Tim set up the overhead projector, Hutton announced, "While I was watching the news this morning, it showed how it took over 100 years for the population to reach one billion and another time it took only 12 years to add another billion. That's a really big difference."

Tim responded, "I'm glad you brought that up; that's exactly what this graph shows. I'll read a bit about it first." Tim read that there is a debate about population growth, and then he asked the students what a debate is, thereby ensuring that the children were familiar with this important democratic process. Lora volunteered "an argument or disagreement." Tim added that there are different opinions about whether the increasing world population poses a threat.

"Some would say that there aren't enough resources now—not enough food or water for everyone. It says here that of the 370,000 people born each day, the majority will be born poor." Tim continued reading, "The population recently increased by 1 billion in just 12 years—that's what Hutton was saying. That means it's increased by one-third since I was in college—think what it will be when you're in college if it keeps increasing at this rate! Some people are concerned that we'll have a hard time producing enough food to feed everybody."

Tim illuminated the graph on the overhead projector and explained, "See, this is what Hutton was talking about. Here is the world population up to the year 1500, and there is still less than a half-billion people." He indicated how the population began to increase more and more sharply up until present times, pointing to the steep ascending line on the graph. "Why do you think the change has increased more rapidly over time?"

Hutton took the pointer and suggested that earlier in time there was no medicine. He moved the pointer along the graph, while saying, "There was more medicine, then more medicine, more medicine, so fewer people were dying. There was less child sicknesses."

Tim responded, "So you think that the development of medicines and medical care improved, and so fewer people died young. That makes sense." Other students suggested other ways that health care has improved over the years, such as the increase in the number of doctors.

Faith placed the pointer to the left portion of the graph and said, "There were fewer people reproducing here and more people reproducing here [moving the pointer to the right side of the graph]."

Tim clarified, "So when there are fewer people, they are not doubling a lot, but when there is a larger number, it doubles a lot more. If it doubles again in four years, think of how much that will be."

Taylor added, "That reminds me of *The King's Chessboard*," a book the class had read with Tim in second grade about doubling grains of rice with each move on a 64-square chessboard, leading

> to tons and tons of rice (Birch, 1988). Tim had actually planned to
> follow up this class discussion by reading that book again, so he
> replied, "Huh, funny you should mention that. What makes you
> think that?" Taylor explained how the population keeps doubling
> much like the grains of rice doubled in that book.
>
> Sarah suggested that 100 years ago people were poorer and
> there were fewer resources for health care. Tim expanded her think-
> ing, asking whether a graph of income would look similar to the
> world population graph. Sarah thought about it and said yes.
>
> Tim added, "A lot of graphs would look like this—food pro-
> duction, for example. Or the average age that people die."

This conversation shows how the class inquired into the meaning of a graph, talking it through to decipher it and asking deeper questions about the world, considering such topics as poverty, hunger, medical care, and food production. Tim often clarified and expanded on the
students' understandings, leading them in a thoughtful and critical discussion of world population growth. Thus the children not only learn
about social issues through the language of graphs and statistics, but
they also learn to dig deeper in their interpretations through these kinds
of discussions.

Looking Closely at Social Issues

One year when Tim was teaching third grade, several statewide debates
were in full swing, including whether to develop a lottery to fund education and to legalize video poker. Children brought in newspaper articles about the controversies and Tim shared letters from the editor
about the issues. He also asked the children to ask their parents about
their opinions on the topics, which they often discussed the following
day. Tim also encouraged them to think about their own points of view
and why they might hold the opinions they have. He is always careful
about not expressing his own opinion on controversial issues because
he doesn't want the students to feel that they have to share his perspective—he genuinely wants them to explore and be able to express their
own opinions.

Once when Tim was reading letters from the editor during news
sharing time, Lora asked if she could write a letter to a senator. Tim responded by distinguishing between writing to a political representa-

tive and writing to the editor of a newspaper. One boy, Tom, suggested that the entire class could write a letter. Tim pointed out that not everybody in the class would necessarily share the same opinion. He suggested that they inquire into class opinions by conducting a class survey and creating a graph that illustrated their different points of view, as they had done several times before on other topics such as "What did you eat for breakfast today?" and "favorite books and authors." Lora decided she would like to write a letter to the editor and asked if the class could have information about doing so. Tim read the instructions directly from the newspaper, and one of the children later printed that information on chart paper. This chart also included information on how to address a senator or representative. It's important to note that Tim never guides students' opinions; he simply provides them with the information they need to exercise their rights and express their voices about social and political matters. In other words, he helps them learn the language and processes for becoming active, vocal citizens.

Throughout this discussion, Tim implicitly indicated to students that he expects people's opinions to differ and that he values those differences. He helps children explore their own opinions and learn to express them through different opportunities. One week, for example, the children busily developed their papers on whether to support the whaling industry. One by one they read their opinions to their classmates, who had the opportunity to discuss each paper in turn. Joseph suggested that he was neither for nor against whaling, that it depended on different circumstances. Tim then highlighted Joseph's example of taking context into account. Children were learning language that helped them uncover and express their points of view by talking and writing about them; these are crucial skills for active citizens in a democracy.

Participating

As teachers, we know that communities don't form overnight or remain static through the rest of the school year. Throughout morning meetings, Tim helps the children learn how to participate in discussions in meaningful and equitable ways. He cultivates responsibilities of participation by:

- offering different forms of turn-taking
- creating student jobs
- supporting student initiative

Turn-Taking

Democracies prosper when all individuals have a voice. As in any group, there will always be those who like to talk more than others. Tim seeks ways to encourage the more silent children to participate more and the more verbal students to reserve talking space for others. When it comes to discussing the topic at hand, the class has tried out a variety of turn-taking strategies, each of which has advantages and disadvantages. Therefore, Tim selects strategies based on his vision of the children's current needs and interests and the nature of the topic under exploration. Early in the school year, Tim calls on students who raise their hands or suggests that they "go around the circle," with each student making a contribution if she or he so chooses. Tim also gives students more opportunities to guide the discussion through various methods. He names the strategies so that the kids know how to respond during any given class conversation and come to recognize different ways of using language in group discussions.

Speaker's Choice. In this method, the person who initiated the topic calls on classmates, teachers, and other adults who have raised their hands. Jack, for example, shared a newspaper article about jellyfish, enthusiastically summarizing the article:

"There are some kinds of jellyfish that haven't been seen in ten years that are coming back. There's a basketball-size kind and another one that has come back that is the size of a platter or something, and their tentacles can reach about 25 feet. And, um, can I go ahead and call on Jonathan?" [who had his hand up].

Tim responded, "Sure, go ahead."

Jonathan offered a personal connection to Jack's news on jellyfish: "When I went to the beach, my mom caught a jellyfish that was like that tall and this wide [gesturing with his hands] and I was, I just buried them so nobody would be able to find them and mess with them."

Jack then went on to share some graphs from the article regarding types of jellyfish. When he finished, Tim suggested, "Call on a few more kids, " then added, "If you can, if you recognize when kids have their hands up that don't usually raise their hands or don't get called on very often, try to call on them."

"Okay," Jack responded, and he called on Chandler.

Chandler shared a story about spotting a jellyfish on the beach that scared his sister. Jack called on Cameron, who asked, "Can any jellyfish get close to the shore?"

"Yeah," responded Jack.

Cameron continued, "What are they called?"

Jack answered, "One that doesn't have a real name, only its scientific name, it gets washed up to the beach all the time and it ruined the vacation for all sorts of people."

Tim eagerly handed over to Jack the responsibility of guiding the discussion. Jack was the expert, taking and responding to questions about the topic of jellyfish. An alternative way for children to guide the discussion is for the person who just made a comment to pick the next speaker. Thus, after Chandler offered his personal connection, he would select the next speaker. Either way, the children, rather than the teacher, guide the conversation. Tim still sees it as his responsibility to help the children distribute turn-taking fairly, as when he reminded Jack to call on children who speak least frequently in discussions.

Fist and Fingers. Tim learned this strategy from Hope Jenkins, a teacher who participated with him in a national videoconference in 1998. It promotes a fair distribution of talk among members of the class. If a person has not made a comment yet and they wish to do so, they hold up a fist. After making a comment, when they want to speak again they hold up one finger, or two fingers if they have already made two comments. Those holding up fists are given priority in speaking. This is a useful strategy for creating equity. It also helps students who are eager to respond to any topic to be judicious in choosing the time to speak. It's an effective strategy if the topic is likely to raise multiple comments from people. Whenever children read an entry about their observation of a class pet, for example, other students are eager to share their observations. They often have personal connections to make, such as the jellyfish stories shared by Jonathan and Chandler. Whenever multiple students are eager to talk, the fist-and-fingers strategy is a good one to use. As with several of these strategies, however, it can be difficult to have an authentic discussion, since somebody might have a response to another person's comment but may not have the opportunity to make it right away, thereby generating a more stilted conversation.

Speak into the Silence. This is a strategy that one of the fifth-grade classes developed a few years ago with their teacher, Rick DuVall (DuVall, 2001). It fosters natural conversation. Rick's class had done an inquiry into how their families managed group conversations, and one student said that his family members of course don't bother raising hands at dinner but instead listen for a pause in the conversation and then "speak into the silence." Many of the classrooms at the Center have embraced this strategy of paying attention to the conversation and making one's comment when there is a natural pause. While this strategy promotes genuine conversation, the children have found that it can be challenging in large-group discussions, particularly when the topic is engaging and lots of kids have something to say about it! Also, some eager students need to be reminded to leave more room for silence before plunging in, give way to another student who wishes to speak, or take a reasonable amount of time taking the floor. Sometimes Tim or other students will remind the class of these expectations if they choose to "speak into the silence."

One of Tim's third-grade classes talked about the meaning of Thanksgiving and compared two picture books they had read. One of the books, *How Many Days to America?* (Bunting, 1988), illustrated the experience of a group of people emigrating from their home country to the United States in a boat. Several children compared this story to the arrival of the Pilgrims. By speaking into the silence, they built on one another's thinking as they pondered some big ideas.

Sarah commented, "I think that the people in this story are more like immigrants since the United States already had Pilgrims living in it."

Tim wondered, "What are Pilgrims? Are Pilgrims not immigrants?"

Sarah thought about it and responded, "Well, sort of, yeah."

"I'm not trying to convince you, but I'm trying to work this out for myself as well," Tim said. "It seems like they are. If you think about the first Pilgrims, they were immigrants to this nation from England, by way of Holland."

Cameron entered the conversation by linking Sarah and Tim's ideas: "I think, at the end of the story, the soldiers helped the immigrants, and in the same way, the Indians helped the Pilgrims."

Sarah then brought all their points together: "I had another connection between Thanksgiving and *How Many Days to America?*, sort of picking up with Cameron's thoughts. When they first came to the land and the people on the boat were scared of the soldiers, like when the Pilgrims first came to America and they were scared of the Indians. But then when the Indians gave the Pilgrims food, they weren't scared of them anymore. When the soldiers gave food to the people coming to America, then they weren't scared of them anymore. They weren't like 'they have guns so maybe they are going to try and shoot us' and things like that."

Tim mused, "Maybe they learned to trust each other."

Tim uses a variety of methods for helping children learn how to take turns fairly and participate in the discussion. Rather than stick to any one strategy, we have found it useful to use a range of strategies for turn-taking; different strategies may be more useful at different times of the school year. In the later part of the year, Tim will often give the choice to students, asking, "How do you want to do this, fist and fingers? Or should we just speak into the silence?" Sometimes he doesn't have to ask, for a student will suggest, "Can we speak into the silence?"

Cynthia Lewis's (2001) research of social practices in one teacher's classroom reminds us that classroom communities are complex social environments—challenging places to create equal access for all students, with no simple solutions. It is important that teachers be attentive to classroom contexts that influence children's participation. We have considered here how, in some small ways, offering a range of turn-taking strategies can encourage different forms of participation. Lewis's work underscores the importance of offering a variety of grouping arrangements as well; depending on the context, some children may be in a better position to voice their points of view in a peer-led discussion rather than a whole-class discussion, for example.

Staying on Topic

Children also develop responsibility for listening carefully to the conversation and making comments that relate to the topic at hand. As teachers know, when a number of children have knowledge to share and each insight leads to another, it is easy to diverge from the topic.

Tim believes that children learn best when they can make personal connections to the topic being discussed. These connections can enrich the conversation and add insight. He also understands that children make sense of their world and share their understandings through stories. Sometimes, however, these connections and stories take on a life of their own. A student sharing a newspaper article about boat safety, for example, led to a string of children eager to tell boat stories of their own, without necessarily tying them into the idea of boat safety.

At such times, Tim needs to be the teacher. In other words, he needs to decide whether the class would benefit from continuing in that direction, returning to the original topic, or moving on to the next activity. As teachers, we know this is a delicate balance. Shall we move the discussion along in order to get to other important parts of the curriculum, or provide space for students to share their stories? Often a compromise is struck, and room is provided for some stories. Tim might, for example, suggest that three more students share their stories, and then he invites the others to share those personal connections and stories in other forums, such as a quick pair-share. Or he might suggest that they write their ideas in the appropriate class journal or their own writer's notebook.

Class Jobs

Another way that children practice responsible participation is through class jobs, which include those typical in many classrooms: watering plants, feeding the class pets, and collecting papers. Several class jobs, however, do allow children to take roles in facilitating class discussions and activities.

One typical morning, Elijah, as timekeeper, used the stopwatch to time the attendance roll call. When Tim called the last name, Elijah hit the stop button on the stopwatch, announcing that it took them 14.35 seconds. Elijah wrote that figure on the whiteboard and then looked at the top of the board to see what was recorded as the class's fastest roll call time to date: 13.48 seconds. He wrote that number under 14.35 and then talked through the subtraction required to determine the difference between that day's roll call time and the fastest time of the year. The messenger, Melissa, then read out the lunch menu and asked students to raise their hand if they were buying lunch. She took the lunch count and attendance papers to the office. When it was time to sing songs, Mahogany was in charge of the random cup. She picked out three names and announced them. Those three children selected the song for the class to sing. Mahogany picked out another name, and Christine was selected to guide the singing by holding a pointer to the lyrics that were written on chart paper.

These jobs are important for helping students take responsibility and ownership of each school day. The jobs are determined collaboratively at the beginning of the year and are rotated every one or two weeks. They may shift over time as Tim or his students recognize a need to create a new job or revise the responsibilities of an existing job.

Student Initiative

By encouraging student participation in conversations through various turn-taking strategies and supporting children's responsibilities through class jobs, Tim fosters student initiative. He encourages the students to suggest classroom strategies and ideas for projects. Starting on the first day of school, Tim works with the children to shape the daily schedule.

They also decide what rituals to include in their daily lives. It was Tim's idea to share news, and he developed the math and science journals. Over time the children and the teacher devise new rituals and engagements. The language journal, for example, developed as a result of a dilemma. One day Mahogany asked why the beige skin of white people was called white. An interesting discussion on the chemistry of skin tone and the cultural labels we affix to skin color followed. Mahogany asked where she should write such a question, for it didn't seem to fit in the science or math journals. And so the language journal was born.

Another day Hutton read his observation from the science journal: "Did you know that the Great Wall of China is so long that you can see it from the moon?" Tim commented, "Hutton has found a new use for the science journal. It isn't just a place to ask questions or write observations, but also to share some facts." Another boy noted that he had heard that this fact about the Great Wall of China was a myth, and the class discussed what resources could confirm this information. Through Hutton's initiative to write not just questions but also facts in the journals, the class also came to see the journal as a place to explore and debate "facts."

Student initiative can lead to new learning engagements. Each morning the children can write, read, or play commercial or student-created board games. As described earlier, Christine introduced her love of chess to the class by playing with Tim each morning. Chess became one of the class's favorite morning activities. In one morning meeting, Sarah raised a concern about the class chessboards. When students had to stop before a game was finished, they would put the board aside with all the pieces in place so that they could resume the game later. Sarah noted her concern and solution: "This happened to me and Christine's board. Somebody had taken our board down from the top of the cubbies and moved the pieces out of place, so we had to start our game over again. So now what you can do is you can get some sticky paper and put your name on it and then put it up." Sarah's solution was taken up and chess games continued uninterrupted. In many ways, then, Tim's room is a place to foster responsibility for taking the initiative to suggest new strategies, ideas, or solutions.

Weaving a Democratic Community through Academic Activities

This chapter looks closely at the processes of democratic knowledge building. As was made clear in earlier chapters, however, Tim develops a democratic class community with his students through inquiry, literacy, and other academic activities throughout the year. Chapter 2, for example, concluded with a scene from the Literacy Club, where children critiqued academic institutions and scientific research institutions. It is important that democratic community building not be separated from the curriculum. As we illustrated in this chapter, it is critical to create with students a curriculum in which all voices can be heard, in which personal knowledge is valued and extended, and in which learners can build knowledge together. Such democratic ways of life are more often a point of departure than a destination. Tim continuously revises his practice as he works toward these democratic ways of living in his classroom. He strives to create a classroom where children learn language with which to collaborate and express their views; it is also a place to use language to begin to explore and critique the very social institutions and practices that we create.

5 Letter from a Teacher

Dear Teachers,

It is with great pleasure that I write you this long note. While I love to write letters, I have never written anything professionally in this voice. For this correspondence with you, I do not need references. For this chapter, I do not need classroom research. I only need to rely on my experience as a teacher. In this context, I am simply writing a letter to a friend and a colleague. I am writing this to you.

For we have common interests. While we may teach in different contexts (for the last seven years, I have been teaching in the school of my dreams, one which I helped to create with like-minded colleagues— how many teachers can say that?), the teaching essentials are the same wherever you go.

This letter is not intended to be advice so much as a reflection on the profession. If 100 teachers were to write such a letter, there would be 100 very different letters. Maybe you should write a letter with your reflections on the teaching profession. Send it to a friend; give it to your teaching team members, your principal, your students' parents, your staff. All of us have important things to say to each other. Who can help us to be better at our craft than other classroom teachers?

The Importance of Peers

I was lucky to have some very good teachers and cooperating teachers in my training. I also had some clunkers, as I'm sure you have. When I was student teaching, my cooperating teacher yelled at her second graders constantly. She threw tantrums in front of the kids. One day she shredded a child's paper and hollered at her for daring to play around with cursive handwriting, for she alone knew when it was time to begin teaching cursive. Any habits children learned on their own would have to be broken when she taught cursive the proper way. According to this teacher, the little girl had a lot of nerve trying something like that on her own, and she had better not catch her doing it again.

I went to my university supervisor and complained that I never wanted to go back into that classroom again.

"You can learn from lousy teachers too," she responded. "If you can stick it out for nine weeks, you'll be stronger." She told me that I could learn how "not to teach" from this experience. I could stand it for only one more day. The constant berating and belittling of children was too much, and I figured I couldn't have much of an impact on the school lives of these children. Call me a coward, but I bailed out. I went back to my supervisor and said that I would do my student teaching the following semester. I didn't mind. Maybe I could work on some courses for my master's degree. I just couldn't learn "how not to teach" from that teacher.

Luck was with me and I ended up working with a wonderful cooperating teacher at the university lab school. Sandy Richards was a master. She loved and respected children. She encouraged them to take risks and to learn from one another. The placement in her room was perfect.

In some ways, I failed the children in my first placement. If I had stuck it out, I might have made a positive difference in the classroom. The teacher might have lightened up a little and tried something new, writing workshop perhaps. I'll never know now. This experience is significant to me in that I realized how important it is to have mentors and colleagues who can truly make a difference in our professional lives. It is hard to be alone and still be strong. It is so important to have colleagues you can run ideas by, brag about your students' accomplishments to, brainstorm and commiserate with. You need someone you can admit your mistakes to, someone to prop you up and to laugh with. If you are lucky, it can be the teacher next door or down the hall. If you are very lucky, you may be involved with an entire staff of like-minded people who can push you, question you, and challenge you. Sometimes it may be difficult to find those special people you can relate to and think creatively and holistically with. Don't give up. Go to professional meetings; join a teacher support group, read professional literature.

Constantly learning "how not to teach" from peers leads to serious burnout. There have been situations in which I was happy enough just to close my door and do the best teaching I could. At the time, I felt that my teaching was going just fine. I may have been considered the odd-fellow-at-the-end-of-the-hall, but it didn't matter. My students were thriving, their parents appreciated what was happening in the classroom, and I could jump through the hoops of the teacher evaluation lessons. I was fine being an island. Or was I? In retrospect, I think I could have been a much better teacher, and, more important, the students might have gotten much more out of school during those years if I had had some teachers to compare notes with. By closing my door, no one could see the fantastic things my students were doing and the discoveries we were making. Going underground in my teaching wasn't really fair to my students, and I wasn't growing as a teacher.

The Power of Our Inquiry

Something else that makes a difference in the lives of students and teachers is for us to be active and sincere learners ourselves. How can we teach kids the importance of recreational reading if we don't make space for it in our classrooms and if we are not readers ourselves? How can we teach writing if we don't write? Don't you know teachers who teach biology, and during the entire study there isn't a living organism in the room other than humans? How do we teach astronomy and never look together at the night sky? How do we teach magnetism and not really know (or care) how it works?

I'm not suggesting that we reinvent the wheel every year. You don't need to start from scratch every time you plan a unit of study. But there does need to be authentic inquiry going on—even for us teachers. Don't simply take down your October box or pull out your animal unit file. Try a new experiment, something you really don't know the outcome to. Try a new field study; invite in a new guest speaker. Be amazed. Don't underestimate the power of your own amazement and its effect on your students. During writing workshop, set aside enough time to enjoy what you ask your students to enjoy. Be more than a model—be a writer.

Children develop trust in what we say when we are brave enough to try out what we are having them do. How many of us consider ourselves to be writers? Scientists? Mathematicians? And yet isn't that what we demand of our students?

Bringing Parents into the Conversation

Initially, I wasn't sure whether this letter was the proper place for a discussion of bringing parents into the classroom; this might not seem like the place to reflect on such an important part of my personal journey as a teacher. Then I considered that, after the children, our next primary concern as teachers is for our students' parents. They know their children better than we ever could. Of course, the time they spend with their children is vital to the children's education. Parents' observations and feedback can make a tremendously positive impact on how we teach and how well we know our students. They have important things to say to us about their children and to other parents.

When I first started out as a teacher, I invited parents into the classroom. In my first newsletter every year and at our open house, I would tell parents that our classroom door was always open to them. They didn't have to tell me in advance if they wanted to come in. Thinking back on these invitations, I'm not sure how sincere they were. Rarely did anyone take me up on the offer. An occasional parent would show up to eat lunch with his or her child, and parents came along on field studies, but they had no real impact on our school days.

Then about twelve years ago a mom took me up on my offer. Anna Inbody showed up at a writing workshop early in the school year with her nine-month-old son and asked what she could do to help. At first I really didn't know what to say. I suggested that she observe and follow the children's and my lead. She was fearless. Soon she was listening to children read their drafts, helping them edit, inviting children to sit in author's circles, and even doing some writing of her own. Her baby, William, was set up on a blanket with some toys and made himself right at home.

Over that school year, Anna and William's visits became a regular part of our week. We all watched as William learned to pull himself up, cruise the classroom by holding on to the edges of desks, and finally walk on his own. When they couldn't come in, we missed them. Anna was there, not just as an assistant but as another editor, organizer, model, writer, and mentor. Anna shared wonderful anecdotes with me that I would have missed had I been the only adult in the room.

The following year at open house I was specific about the need to have parents participate. I requested that parents sign up and asked that they commit to coming in at least once during the year to be a part of our workshop even if it meant taking an early lunch one day or some time away from their jobs. I asked our room mother to try to schedule at least one parent for each workshop. Not everyone came, of course, but many parents did. Their participation made a wonderful difference in the quality of our workshop time. Since that year with Anna and William, I have always tried to include parents in this important time in our schedule.

Not all parents can come into the classroom, of course. In many homes, both parents work and cannot get away even for a morning. Many children come from single-parent homes, so parent participation in school activities is virtually impossible. Therefore, our parent newsletters became a way for all parents to become involved in their children's literacy.

Parent Newsletters: Sharing Ideas and Making Voices Heard

This section of my letter to you contains some of my letters to parents this year—letters within a letter. The letters *you* write to parents would be very different. You could never use these in your correspondence to parents. If you chose to write similar letters, they would be personal and reflect what is happening in your classroom and in the lives of your students.

The newsletter isn't a novel idea. Teachers have been writing great letters to parents for far longer than I have been a teacher. A thoughtful newsletter takes time and effort to put together, but you get a tremendous return on your investment. Over the years, my letters have changed in format and content. My early ones were handwritten, then I began typing them (with lots of whiteout), and now, of course, they are created on the computer. In some ways, they have become more complicated, but still they remain letters. Letter writing is something of a lost art in these days of e-mail and short, tersely worded memos. Letter writing is personal. Letters contain an inherent sincerity that often isn't found in other forms of communication. I try to keep the personal voice alive in my letters to parents. After looking at a file of letters, I distilled this list of benefits from sending letters home to parents:

- The letters inform parents about areas of curriculum we are examining in the classroom: units of study, projects, due dates, etc.
- They make conferencing easy. Parents are well informed about their child's academic strengths and areas that need attention.
- The newsletters help to develop and share a vision of literacy.
- They foster genuine conversation through writing. They give parents a voice in their children's classroom.
- Parents become more effective teachers.
- By participating in our newsletter projects, parents build a repertoire of activities to do at home.
- They encourage quality time between parents and children.
- Parents inform the curriculum through their responses to newsletter projects.
- When their responses are printed in subsequent newsletters, parents inform other parents about how to work with their children and how to become better kidwatchers.
- Parents assist with evaluation and record keeping through their participation in projects and written observations.
- The letters solidify the relationship between parents and teachers.
- They encourage individualized instruction and tutoring.

- They allow teachers and parents to share their philosophies of education.

- They inform parents of best practice in education.

I used to think it was very important to keep a file of letters I've sent home so that I could just pull up last year's letters and do a little editing, cutting, and pasting and I'd have a ready supply of newsletters for the next year. In fact, I have never been able to reuse old letters, for obvious reasons. The newsletters are different from year to year because the students are different; what is happening in the classroom and in the world is different.

Something that my more recent letters have in common is that I have tried to give parents more of a voice. Often I reproduce their responses to questions and their children's work right in subsequent letters. In this way, parents can inform each other and me.

Many of my newsletters contain invitations for parents to work on a project with their child, from listening to their child read and having a written conversation about a story, to creating a graph, to editing a story together from writing workshop. I include as options a cross section of the kinds of projects and activities we do in school. For every one of these instructional invitations, I ask parents to write a note to me about how they think their child is doing. Their notes become important information for me because they know their child better than I could ever hope to. Parents are the ultimate kidwatchers.

Discussing Literacy through Newsletters

Another relevant change in my letters is that I now invite parents to share their insights about the literacy questions we are pondering in the classroom. The focus of the following selection of letters is just that. With my new class of second graders this year, I focused largely on *strategies* as a way of becoming more proficient readers. It was essential for us to define reading and to think about what processes are involved. After the children read and examined their own reading processes, they generated a list of strategies they had used. In the following newsletter, I included this information for parents:

[Excerpt from 9/25/02 newsletter]

We spent a lot of time last week coming up with a list of reading strategies. Since the beginning of the year we have been exploring the question, *"What is reading?"* The short answer we have come up with is, *"Reading is understanding. Reading is making sense."* As I read with children individually and in small groups I notice what they do to *understand* and *make sense* of what they are reading. I have been sharing the strategies I see and children have been sharing their ideas as well. Here is a list of reading strategies we have come up with so far. The best readers use many of these while reading. It is important to understand that *"sounding out"* is only one of many strategies that we use to understand what we read. Young readers seem to use letter sounds more often while more experienced readers rely more on strategies which involve using the context to make useful predictions.

Reading Strategies

- If something doesn't make sense, read it again.
- Point to the words or use an underliner to keep your spot.
- Read on, then come back and look at the letters and think of words that would make sense that look like that word.
- Ask someone for help.
- Use what you know about letter patterns (silent "e" means long vowel, two vowels together makes a long vowel).
- Break up the word into parts, sound out the parts, put it back together.
- Use the letter sounds. Say them slowly, then say the word quickly.
- Read past the word. Come back to the word with more clues from the rest of the sentence.
- Look for word parts that you do know.
- Cover word parts, focus on other word parts, and put the parts together.
- Skip names that are hard or say them your own way.
- Use the pictures to help you.
- Use what you know about suffixes (word endings) and prefixes (word beginnings).
- Use the meaning of the story to make predictions.
- Substitute another word that makes sense.

This is a pretty sophisticated list of strategies and I'm sure we will add to these as the year goes by. The most important thing to remember is that *reading is understanding.* So, even the strategy that suggests sounding out words is only useful if one sounds out words to *understand.* This list may be important to you as you coach your child.

After giving parents a week to consider these strategies, in the next newsletter I asked the parents to write down their ideas about what they do when they read.

[Excerpt from 10/3/02 newsletter]

I'd like to get some of your ideas to add to our list of strategies. Please consider this question, *"What do you do when you are reading and you come to a new or difficult word or passage?"* Over the weekend when you pick up a novel, recipe, newspaper, or set of instructions, think about what you do to make sense of what you are reading. Take just a minute to examine what you do when you read and share some of your strategies with us. You probably do many of the same things we have on our list but you may help us out by thinking of something we haven't considered.

I received many responses to this question, and we discussed all of them in class. It was good for the children to know that how they read closely matches how their parents read. A few weeks later I printed parents' responses in the newsletter:

[Excerpt from 10/24/02 newsletter]

I want to thank all of the parents who responded to my question a few weeks ago about reading strategies. Many of the strategies reported by parents mirror the ones we have already discussed in class. The question was, "What do you do when you come to a difficult word or passage?" The answers ranged from the very simple . . . *"Ask my wife,"* to the very complicated . . . *"When I'm reading technical computer language—if the context is not enough, then I try other strategies."* Many of the strategies mentioned by parents have to do with using the context of the passage to make sense of the difficult sections . . . *"Read the sentence or passage that comes before and after the difficult word. . . . Reread the sentence or paragraph to see if I understand it better. . . . I usually try to guess what it means based on how it's used. . . ."* Some of you said that you would look up the word, *"I use the dictionary ASAP. It drives me crazy <u>not</u> to know what a word means."* Several said that they examine the word parts, *"Bio-ology = 'life' and 'the study of' . . . look for the root word. . . . Break up the information into smaller segments and try to understand the smaller segments."*

Only a few parents mentioned sounding out words as a way of understanding the text. It's interesting to note that the primary strategy we use to teach young ones to read is using the letter sounds, but it seems to be a last resort for most of us. If you think about it, we don't sound out much. I say all of this to encourage you to use what you know about reading when you coach your young reader. If you are a good reader yourself, if you enjoy reading and spend time reading for pleasure, then you already know a lot about the process. Think about <u>***what you do***</u> when you read and use that information to help your child. We fall back on *"sound it out"* when we give advice to children when we don't use that strategy very often ourselves.

I also took the opportunity to solicit parents' responses about the qualities of good writing:

[Excerpt from 11/15/02 newsletter]

On Monday, during independent reading, I asked the children to write down a favorite passage they read. Everyone shared examples they found of great writing. Afterwards I asked the children to describe some of the characteristics of great writing. We came up with a list that, to me, is quite remarkable.

What is WELL CRAFTED writing?

- You love to talk about it and share it with others. You hope they will read it too.
- It is something you remember for a long time.
- It makes you forget where you are and forget about time when you are reading it.
- It changes you—maybe forever. You feel it in your heart.
- It teaches you facts, morals, how to behave. . . .
- It can be emotional. It makes you FEEL.
- You want to read on. You don't want to put it down.
- It can make you laugh, or smile, or cry ("tears of joy"). It is descriptive and clear. The words are well chosen.
- You want to read it again.
- You can put yourself there.
- It invites predictions.
- It invites connections (text-to-text, text-to-world, and text-to-self).
- It can be sad, happy, mysterious, funny, informative, surprising, exciting, touching. . . .

I invite you to share some of your ideas with us about what makes something great writing. We enjoyed your reading strategies and discussed every one in class.

In the next letter, I asked parents to respond to the question about qualities of great writing in a more formal way with another questionnaire:

Consider what you like to read. Think about your favorite books and authors. Think about letters or cards you have received that really moved you. Think about instruction manuals, newspaper and magazine articles, trade journals, and anything else that you enjoy reading. Please list qualities that you feel are important for good writing.

Parents rose to the occasion by writing thoughtful responses. I took the opportunity to let them teach and learn from each other in the newsletter:

[Excerpt from 12/12/02 newsletter]

I like for books and letters to give me a sense of being at the setting being written about . . . to provide a perspective for the characters. What is their history? . . . Writing so your audience feels like you're sitting there talking to them. . . . Writing using your 5 senses. . . . [A] "page-turner" that you can't put down—and don't want to until you're finished with the book. . . . Well organized and logical. . . . A good story is told from the right point of view with just the right details included. . . . Interesting with good descriptive words. . . . Good writing has to touch the heart. . . . Know your audience. . . .

David's dad, a Chinese American, wrote so nicely about the subject that I want to include what he wrote in his own words.

[Emotion—You will cry or laugh or feel angry or feel happy while reading a book.

Inspiration—It inspires you to do good and great things. It inspires you to dream big.

Imagination—It talks about people or things that you would hardly think of.

Knowledge—Using well-organized structure and logic to teach you complicated things.

Beauty—You feel the beauty of writing and you want to read over and over to enjoy the beauty the writing presents.]

I am often asked if there are parents who choose not to participate in the newsletter invitations. Of course some parents choose not to participate. I'm sure some parents do not read the letters carefully, if at all. All we can do is our best to invite parents in. Some parents feel they are too busy to deal with the day-to-day education of their children. Some parents have so much pressure to provide for their family that responding to their children's newsletter is the furthest thing from their minds. I do not blame parents for not being really active in their responses. But I still put the call out there as a true invitation.

I strive to communicate to parents that I value the quality and sincerity of their comments. Parents soon come to realize that I care about the content of our correspondence and not the mechanical correctness. Consequently, most parents of diverse backgrounds have chosen to join in this written correspondence over time.

Reading Logs: Another Part of the Literacy Conversation

For several years, I have asked my students to read for a certain amount of time each day as part of their homework. I call it recreational reading because they can choose whatever they want to read. It began when a pizza restaurant chain offered pizza parties as a bonus for children who read for a required amount of time. The kids who kept up with the record forms and got their parents to sign each week were rewarded with a pizza party at the end of the school year. The ones who didn't do the reading or didn't keep up with the record keeping part of the task got no party. The system was pretty cut and dried. I never took to the pizza party part of the project, but I liked the idea of asking the children to read as a regular part of their homework. I created my own form for the children to use to record the amount of time they read each week. I also asked that parents sign the form at the end of the week.

For several years, this seemed to work. Occasionally I tallied the collective number of minutes read by the class and reported the results in the newsletter, congratulating everyone on a job well done. I was aware that many of the forms were obviously filled out at the last minute, probably on the morning the reading log was due. I also figured that some of the children were not being entirely honest about the amount of time they spent reading and that parents were, in some cases, covering for the kids by signing the forms even though much of the reported reading probably wasn't done.

After a while, I began to ask the children to write a little about what they had read during the week. I figured this would keep them honest and would work in a little real writing. These writing responses were usually outstanding at the beginning of every year and then dwindled off into obligatory responses that were not very thoughtful by midyear. In retrospect, these responses became mere tasks to complete and, aside from the possible benefit of the children being able to select their own reading material and logging in their times, they were pretty worthless. At the time, however, I continued to feel that this strategy was a success, if only because the children were reading a lot. Why? Because I required it!

I'm not sure why it took me so long, but this year I finally began to use the reading logs as a tool to generate larger conversations about books. I guess you *can* teach an old dog new tricks. I was determined to have a reading log that was interactive, one that invited parents into the conversation (beyond merely signing off on the form). This year I think home reading finally worked. To begin with, I asked parents to make a commitment to listen to their child read at least once each week. I set up the reading logs through a newsletter explaining the importance of home reading and the parents' role in this important project:

[8/19/03 newsletter]

Today is the first day of our new *Reading Log*. We have discussed this at length and the children should definitely know what is expected. I wanted to give you the information as well, especially since you will play an important role.

I am asking that the children read for at least 15 minutes each day, for at least 5 days per week. I know that there are some who will read for more than this (you could probably guess that I feel the more reading, the better). The children should record the title and author of what they read on the form. I am also asking that they write a response to what was read. We practiced in class last week. Anything they write that tells about what was read will be fine.

Your help may be needed to keep track of the time spent reading. There is a place for this on the form along with a line for your signature. I'd like for you to sign the form every day indicating that you are aware of the time spent reading. You may also want to read over your child's written response.

I probably should say a few words about writing conventions at this point (capitalization, handwriting, punctuation and . . . yes . . . spelling). At this point, I am very accepting of the children's writing just as it is. We should encourage them to write down their thoughts *the best they can*. We want them to be comfortable with writing *what they think* and not just *what they can spell correctly*. So we accept first drafts on these. However, this may also be a good place to do a little instruction if you want to and you feel that your child is ready. Please don't have your child correct these (as in write them over). The idea behind the *Reading Logs* is for everyone to spend some time reading and thinking and writing about what they have read. If you want to work on conventions, try mentioning one or two things such as, *Did you think of capital letters for the beginning of your sentences?* Or, *That has a long "a" sound, right? There must be a silent "e" on the end of the word.*

I am going to ask for another favor on these reading logs, but I really feel that it will be time well spent. I'd like for you to spend at least 15 minutes each week listening to your child read and writing a little note to me with your observations. There is a space on the back of the sheet to record some of your thoughts. I'd like to read *anything* you want to tell me about what you notice about your child as a reader. Here are some questions to consider:

- Does my child enjoy reading?
- Is my child choosing appropriate books?
- Is he/she comfortable discussing what was just read?
- What are some of the strategies my child uses when reading new or unfamiliar words?
- What can I tell about my child by his/her miscues ("mistakes")?
- Does he/she understand what was read?
- What do I know about my child as a reader?

Your insights will help me to know your child as a reader. This is important to help me be a more effective teacher of reading.

Because this is so important to me, I'd like for you to sign the form below and return it so I can tell that you have read this note and that you agree to listen to your child read and respond at least one time each week. If for some reason you don't get around to the *Reading Log* every single week—NO PROBLEM! If you feel uncomfortable with this agreement let me know and we can discuss it.

I feel strongly that *you* are your child's most important teacher. This is especially true when the children are young. I read with each child for about 10 minutes and it took me over a week. If you will read with your child and do some coaching, it will make a tremendous difference. The quality time you spend reading and discussing literature is essential.

There are other ways to be a good reading coach as well. Read to your child. 2nd graders are definitely not too old for bedtime stories. This will give you the opportunity to share favorite stories from your own childhood. Talk about what you are reading for pleasure. Set aside a special time for reading and book talks. Share some of your strategies for what you do when you come to an unfamiliar word. In short, MODEL good reading habits. If reading is obviously important to you, it will have a positive effect on your child.

Please return the form below as soon as you can or contact me with questions and concerns. Thanks in advance for all of your support and guidance.

The results of home reading this year have been great. The biggest difference is the interaction. I respond to the children's reading logs as often as I can. I would like to say I do so every week, but the reality is a little short of that. When I pass the logs back to the class each week, I set aside quiet time for the children to read my responses. In this way, the reading logs become brief written conversations about literature. Every time a parent writes in the comment section, I respond to these as well. Not all responses are entirely positive, but all of them show that parents care about their children's literacy development. Many parents had not done much reading coaching before.

My comments to parents range from agreeing with them on their observations, answering questions about what is developmentally appropriate, giving advice, suggesting books to read and ways to respond to problems, etc. We have developed a kind of writing relationship about the children's literacy development.

I also report parent responses from the comment section in newsletters so parents can coach each other on positive ways to respond to children's reading and writing:

[Excerpt from 8/29/03 newsletter]

Thank you for doing your part. Your responses on the reading logs were very informative. They demonstrate that you know your children well as readers. Here are a few of the parent comments on the logs from last week:

> Her reading is well done with pauses and emphasis carefully placed. . . . Once she slowed down, she got almost every word . . . . She is a good reader. She can explain what she reads. . . . She started to like chapter books and I see she chose several from the library last week. . . . She has to read sentences out loud several times before she gets the context. . . . I would probably choose harder books for him. However, I think he needs to read these easier books for now because they help build his confidence. . . . She does use the pictures to help her figure out the story. . . . He enjoys the story and often substitutes words when unsure instead of sounding out. . . . She sounds very confident and mature in her reading. . . . I have long felt that listening to someone read is very important, so I started reading the Harry Potter books to him last year. Sometimes he would get so excited that he would pick up the books and start reading them on his own—which is exactly what I hoped would happen.

> Someone asked if it was appropriate for _all_ of the children's reading to be done aloud. While it is important to listen to children read so we can be effective coaches, we still want them to develop their "inner reading voice." This can only be done with time spent reading quietly. One very effective way you can continue to coach is discussing the reading with your child.

The important difference is that now we are all communicating and helping each other know what is best for children. Parents appreciate knowing that their input is valued, and children are reading and writing for a purpose other than task completion. I come to know parents and children in a way I otherwise would not. Like the newsletters, being reading coaches gives parents a sense of presence in the classroom. It is truly a win–win situation.

I'll end this lengthy section on parent involvement by making the point that we are at our best when we are not working alone or even parallel with parents and home life. Our job includes blurring the distinction between "the real world" and school for children. School *should be* part of children's real world, and that is a world that includes family. There will always be parents with a hands-off attitude toward school. That doesn't mean they love or care for their children any less than more active parents. Perhaps it is an indication that we need to try even harder to help them see the advantage of their involvement. At any rate, we owe it to ourselves and to the children to make the most of the involvement parents are willing to share with us.

Finding Balance

There is no shortage of sources of stress in teaching. For me, one of the main sources of stress is knowing what strains my students are under. We cannot help taking on the problems of our best friends. The death of loved ones, parents splitting up or losing jobs, and health problems all find their way into our classrooms. Helping children deal with trauma comes with the territory of teaching. It takes a lot of energy to be there for children when they need nurturing. But think of the stress involved in *not* being there for your students when they need a friend or an advocate. The knowledge that your care and friendship have helped make someone's life more comfortable can be the counterweight to the stress that comes with this responsibility.

The teacher's life is necessarily a busy one. I suspect this is particularly true for inquiry teachers who don't rely on textbooks and scope-and-sequence charts to plan curriculum. We find ourselves constantly planning and replanning when things go in a direction different from the one we anticipated. We are constantly gathering text sets, reading over student work, providing written feedback, communicating with parents, writing curriculum, etc. Teaching responsively is taxing. It is similar to performing seven hours a day, only you don't have your lines memorized. But think of what your life would be like if you weren't planning with and for your students. Imagine if you had absolutely no say in what went on in your room. So the stress of being *on* for so long each day may be balanced by knowing how miserable you would be if you had to teach using someone else's agenda entirely.

Stress also comes from the pressure placed on teachers to do the kinds of things in our classrooms we know are contrary to our knowledge of how children learn best. High-stakes tests are probably one of the primary examples of this kind of stress. While tests are improving overall, we still have to help prepare children to demonstrate their knowledge in ways that are, at best, artificial and hardly a true reflection of knowledge or ability. By helping children prepare for standardized tests, we may not be doing our very best teaching. But we must find a balance between what we need to teach in order for our students to be successful in these situations and the kind of teaching that is truly responsive to the needs and interests of children. The truth of the situation is that our students need to do well on this kind of testing for their own sake. It would not be fair to them if we didn't take the time to adequately prepare them for this reality. Hopefully, if the tests are valid, rigorous writing workshops and authentic literature discussions will reflect higher scores. Still, we need to be sure that children can demonstrate what they know in this artificial testing situation. Not to prepare them for the reality of high-stakes tests would do them a great disservice. So we must find a balance for their sake as well as our own.

Karen Smith (1998) talks of test taking as a genre study. If one knows about the genre and is aware of the expectations, the chances of success are increased. One way to prepare for tests is to go through practice exercises. I preface these exercises with remarks like, "I know this is not real reading and writing. Real reading is for pleasure and for learning. These are not real stories. Real stories make you laugh and make you cry. Real stories make you proud that you have learned something. Real stories are more than just a few lines long. Good stories make you want to try some of the things the author has done. Real writing is communication. Real reading and writing are exciting. I want you to know that *I know* this isn't real reading and writing. When we finish with these reading and writing exercises, we'll get back to the real thing. In the meantime, it is important for us to show ourselves, our parents, our principal, and our school board that we know how to read and write. There may be better ways to do this, but for now this is all we have."

I know that if I don't do a good job of preparing my students for the standardized tests, I won't have a job. Is that just a cop-out? A way to relieve myself of the stress and guilt of having to do something that is far from my best teaching? If it is, I can live with that. I am an advocate of authentic assessment. But simply whining and ignoring the tests doesn't do anyone any good, least of all the children.

Many teachers must submit lesson plans that may not be deviated from. In some settings, every teacher in a grade level is expected to teach the same things at the very same time (including being on the very same page of textbooks) in a regimen that, by its very design, rules out creativity and responsive teaching. The push for time on-task in some districts has done away with recess even for very young children. In the name of accountability, some teachers must list standards on the board for every single lesson, and students are expected to know what standard they are working on at any given time. The list goes on and on, and, depending on what region of the country you live in, what state and district, your list of pressures about what and how you teach may be even greater than the ones I've mentioned.

The obvious question is, "Accountable to whom?" We so often know better than the ones creating the rules. If we are accountable to anyone, it is to our students and their parents. Of course, we can't make *any* difference if we lose our jobs by simply refusing to follow our directives. I'm not suggesting civil disobedience, which would get you fired. But I do think that this source of stress is greatly relieved when we *do something about measures that disregard what we know about best practice.* That may mean voicing your concerns at faculty meetings, making an appointment with your curriculum coordinator, volunteering to be on textbook adoption committees, asking questions at school board meetings, and being proactive by participating in the creation of curriculum standards in your district and state. There are ways to change the system. Grumbling alone rarely makes a positive difference.

The reality of teaching is that we are alone in our classrooms with a group of friends, trying to find the most exciting ways to learn and to show what we have learned. We have to strike a balance between what and how we are *expected* to teach and what we know in our hearts we *must* teach. As teachers we have to do all kinds of things that may not be to our liking. But at the heart of every debate about lesson plan forms, standards, curriculum guidelines, high-stakes tests, and basal readers is the best interest of our students. We will always hear comments like "That is what the school board requires. . . . It wasn't that way when I was a child. . . . The standards must guide the curriculum. . . . " This is not new.

Healthy teachers make the best of these situations. We find ways to get real books into the hands of our students. We *will* have authentic conversations in our classrooms. Our classrooms *will* look and feel different from year to year because our students are different, the world is different, and we learn more about how to teach.

Why Teach?

If you are a teacher, you are not in this business for the money or the prestige. Contrary to public sentiment, you are not a teacher for the vacations. You didn't choose to become a teacher for fame or glory (although there is certainly glory in knowing that you helped someone find his or her voice as a writer, or dried someone's tears, or shed some light on the reading process for parents trying to help their children learn to read).

It takes a certain kind of person to become a good teacher. You are selfless. You are a learner. You do the single most important job there is. Yet, beyond your family, classroom, and school, you are probably underappreciated.

People far removed from teaching and learning make important decisions about instruction for their own personal, political, or economic agendas. You deal with that and you make the best of situations that are far from perfect (or sometimes even remotely logical). You deal with the personal problems and concerns of your students but also, in a very real way, the problems of our nation and the world. Who among us didn't help a group of young people, other people's children, try to deal with and make sense of the events of 9/11?

Because we teach children, we affect the future in a very real way. Every life we touch in our classrooms touches the lives of countless others in an echo that sounds into the future further than we could ever know. Someone taught Gandhi and Martin Luther King Jr. and John F. Kennedy how to read and write. You and I are teaching someone right now who might find the cure for AIDS, or who might help negotiate a peaceful settlement in a war, or who might grow up to be a volunteer in a homeless shelter or a nurturing parent. The world is indeed a better place because of what you do. Never lose sight of your contributions.

To Do List

Be humble—be a learner—get to really know your students—be kind—be gentle—be firm—set high expectations—be authentic—don't be a slave to a program or a method—put kids before programs—laugh out loud in class—cry out loud in class—share your favorite books—don't be afraid to make mistakes—learn from your mistakes—avoid making the same mistakes over and over—be best friends with your students—brag about your students—eat lunch with your students—be sure you have colleagues with whom you can brainstorm productively—don't talk down to your kids—stand up for what is right—find the balance between what you have to do and what you should do—give good feedback to your students—let kids know who you really are—use the standards (textbooks, curriculum guides, teaching directives, scope-and-sequence charts, long-range plans, etc.); don't be used by them—teach something different—be amazed—teach something familiar differently—follow your nose—follow your students' lead—read during SSR—write and publish during writing workshop—sing (even if it's off-key)—dance (even if you have no rhythm)—give hugs—receive hugs—love your students—tell your students that you love them—raise your voice only if it's absolutely necessary—play on the recess field with your kids—get a life—get coached by someone you respect—be gracious when you receive constructive criticism—let kids solve most of their own problems—compromise (but not when it comes to the welfare of your kids)—pick your battles carefully—have your kids create the curriculum with you—be respectful of children—say you're sorry when you make a mistake (and mean it)—let your kids know that you are human.

References

Works Cited

Allen, J. (Ed.). (1999). *Class actions: Teaching for social justice in elementary and middle school.* New York: Teachers College Press.

Allington, R. L. (2001). *What really matters for struggling readers: Designing research-based programs.* New York: Longman.

Anderson, C. (2000). *How's it going? A practical guide to conferring with student writers.* Portsmouth, NH: Heinemann.

Ayers, W. (1993). *To teach: The journey of a teacher.* New York: Teachers College Press.

Banks, J. A. (1995). Multicultural education: Historical development, dimensions, and practice. In J. A. Banks & C. A. McGee Banks (Eds.), *Handbook of research on multicultural education* (pp. 3–24). New York: Simon & Schuster Macmillan.

Beane, J. A., & Apple, M. W. (1995). The case for democratic schools. In M. W. Apple & J. A. Beane (Eds.), *Democratic schools.* Alexandria, VA: Association for Supervision and Curriculum Development.

Becker, T. L., & Couto, R. A. (Eds.). (1996). *Teaching democracy by being democratic.* Westport, CT: Praeger.

Beyer, L. E. (Ed.). (1996). *Creating democratic classrooms: The struggle to integrate theory and practice.* New York: Teachers College Press.

Burke, C. (1996). Presentation to teacher researchers at the "Learning to See What's There" Teacher as Researcher conference at the University of South Carolina, Columbia.

Cambourne, B. (1988). *The whole story: Natural learning and the acquisition of literacy in the classroom.* Auckland, New Zealand: Ashton Scholastic.

Cambourne, B. (2003, July). *The Conditions of Learning Workshop.* Presentation for South Carolina Reading Initiative literacy coaches, Governor's Institute of Reading, State Department of Education, Columbia, SC.

Dahl, K. L., Scharer, P., Lawson, L., & Grogan, P. (2001). *Rethinking phonics: Making the best teaching decisions.* Portsmouth, NH: Heinemann.

DeFord, D. E. (1981). Literacy: Reading, writing and other essentials. *Language Arts, 58*(6), 652–58.

Dewey, J. (1938/1963). *Experience and education.* New York: Macmillan.

DuVall, R. (2001). Refining and expanding our notions of inquiry, talk and classroom community. In H. Mills & A. Donnelly (Eds.), *From the ground up: Creating a culture of inquiry.* Portsmouth, NH: Heinemann.

Edelsky, C. (1994). Education for democracy. *Language Arts, 71,* 252–57.

Egawa, K., & Harste, J. C. (Guest Eds.). (2001). What do we mean when we say we want our children to be literate? [Themed issue]. *School Talk, 7*(1).

Fletcher, R., & Portalupi, J. (2001). *Writing workshop: The essential guide.* Portsmouth, NH: Heinemann.

Fountas, I. C., & Pinnell, G. S. (2001). *Guiding readers and writers, grades 3–6: Teaching comprehension, genre, and content literacy.* Portsmouth, NH: Heinemann.

Freire, P. (1970/1995). *The pedagogy of the oppressed.* New York: Seabury Press.

Freire, P. (1973/1998). *Education for critical consciousness.* New York: Continuum.

Goodman, J., with Kuzmic, J., & Wu, X. (1992). *Elementary schooling for critical democracy.* Albany: State University of New York Press.

Goodman, Y. (1978). Kidwatching: An alternative to testing. *National Elementary School Principle, 57*(4), 41–45.

Greene, M. (1988). *The dialectic of freedom.* New York: Teachers College Press.

Greene, M. (1995). *Releasing the imagination: Essays on the education, the arts, and social change.* San Francisco: Jossey-Bass.

Gutmann, A. (1999). *Democratic education.* Princeton, NJ: Princeton University Press.

Hahn, M. L. (2002). *Reconsidering read-aloud.* Portland, ME: Stenhouse.

Halliday, M. A. K. (1975). *Learning how to mean: Explorations in the development of language.* London: Edward Arnold.

Harste, J. (2002, March). *Literacy as inquiry.* Presentation for the South Carolina Reading Initiative, Governor's Institute of Reading, State Department of Education, Columbia, SC.

Harwayne, S. (2001). *Writing through childhood: Rethinking process and product.* Portsmouth, NH: Heinemann.

Hindley, J. (1996). *In the company of children.* Portland, ME: Stenhouse.

Jennings, L. (2000). Academic rigor and moral education: The combination for teaching character. *Teacher Education Journal of South Carolina,* 44–47.

Jennings, L. B. (2001). Inquiry for professional development and continuous school renewal. In H. Mills and A. Donnelly (Eds.), *From the ground up: Creating a culture of inquiry* (pp. 33–54). Portsmouth, NH: Heinemann.

Jennings, L. B., with O'Keefe, T. (2002). Parents, children, and teachers inquiring together: Written conversations about social justice. *Language Arts, 79*(5), 404–14.

Jennings, L., & Green, J. (1999). Locating democratic and transformative practices in classroom discourse. *Journal of Classroom Interaction, 34*(2), i–iv.

Jennings, L., Karvonen, M., Kjervfe, T., Mills, H., & Ness, J. (2003, April). *Examining literacy and inquiry practices within and across classrooms: Findings from a six-year study.* Paper presented at the American Educational Research Association, Chicago, IL.

Jennings, L., O'Keefe, T., & Shamlin, M. (1999). Creating spaces for classroom dialogue: Co-constructing democratic classroom practices in first and second grade. *Journal of Classroom Interaction, 34*(2), 1–16.

Jones, C. (2003). Classroom structures and strategies for comprehensive literacy instruction. *South Carolina English Language Arts Curriculum Standards.* Columbia, SC: South Carolina Department of Education.

Keene, E. O., & Zimmermann, S. (1997). *Mosaic of thought: Teaching comprehension in a reader's workshop.* Portsmouth, NH: Heinemann.

Lewis, C. (2001). *Literary practices as social acts: Power, status and cultural norms in the classroom.* Mahwah, NJ: Erlbaum.

Lindfors, J. W. (1999). *Children's inquiry: Using language to make sense of the world.* New York: Teachers College Press.

Mills, H. (2001a). Epilogue. In H. Mills & A. Donnelly (Eds.), *From the ground up: Creating a culture of inquiry.* Portsmouth, NH: Heinemann.

Mills, H., with Jennings, L. B., Donnelly, A., & Mueller, L. Z. (2001b). When teachers have time to talk: The value of curricular conversations. *Language Arts, 79,* 20–28.

Mills, H., & Donnelly, A. (Eds.). (2001). *From the ground up: Creating a culture of inquiry.* Portsmouth, NH: Heinemann.

Mills, H., O'Keefe, T., & Stephens, D. (1992). *Looking closely.* Urbana, IL: National Council of Teachers of English.

Mills, H., O'Keefe, T., & Whitin, D. J. (1996). *Mathematics in the making: Authoring ideas in primary classrooms.* Portsmouth, NH: Heinemann.

Moustafa, M. (1997). *Beyond traditional phonics: Research discoveries and reading instruction.* Portsmouth, NH: Heinemann.

National Council of Teachers of English and International Reading Association. (1996). *Standards for the English language arts.* Urbana, IL/Newark, DE: Authors.

Noddings, N. (1984). *Caring: A feminine approach to ethics and moral education.* Berkeley: University of California Press.

O'Keefe, T. (1997). The habit of kidwatching. *School Talk, 3*(2), 4–5.

O'Keefe, T. (2001). Giving children voice: Daily rituals that support learning through conversations. In H. Mills & A. Donnelly (Eds.), *From the ground up: Creating a culture of inquiry* (pp. 78–103). Portsmouth, NH: Heinemann.

Owocki, G., & Goodman, Y. (2002). *Kidwatching: Documenting children's literacy development.* Portsmouth, NH: Heinemann.

Peterson, R. (1992). *Life in a crowded place: Making a learning community.* Portsmouth, NH: Heinemann.

Peterson, R., & Eeds, M. (1990). *Grand conversations: Literature groups in action.* New York: Scholastic.

Pierce, K. (1999, November). *Creating classrooms for inquiry.* Paper presented at the National Council of Teachers of English Annual Convention, Denver, CO.

Portalupi, J., & Fletcher, R. (2001). *Nonfiction craft lessons: Teaching information writing K–8.* Portland, ME: Stenhouse.

Ray, K. W. (1999). *Wondrous words: Writers and writing in the elementary classroom.* Urbana, IL: National Council of Teachers of English.

Ray, K. W. (2002). *What you know by heart: How to develop curriculum for your writing workshop.* Portsmouth, NH: Heinemann.

Rosen, H. (1985). *Stories and meaning.* Sheffield, England: National Association for the Teaching of English.

Rosenblatt, L. M. (1995). *Literature as exploration* (5th ed.). New York: Modern Language Association.

Routman, R. (2003a). *Literacy essentials.* Presentation at the Reading Essentials Conference, South Carolina Reading Initiative, Governor's Institute of Reading, State Department of Education, Columbia, SC.

Routman, R. (2003b). *Reading essentials: The specifics you need to teach reading well.* Portsmouth, NH: Heinemann.

Rowe, D. (1986.) *Literacy in the child's world: Preschoolers' explorations of alternate sign systems.* Unpublished doctoral dissertation, Indiana University, Bloomington.

Shor, I. (1992). *Empowering education: Critical teaching for social change.* Chicago: University of Chicago Press.

Short, K. G. (1996). *Learning together through inquiry: From Columbus to integrated curriculum.* York, ME: Stenhouse.

Short, K. G. (1997). *Literature as a way of knowing.* York, ME: Stenhouse.

Short, K. G., & Harste, J. C., with Burke, C. (1996). *Creating classrooms for authors and inquirers* (2nd ed.). Portsmouth, NH: Heinemann.

Smith, F. 1981. Demonstrations, engagement and sensitivity: A revised approach to language learning. *Language Arts, 58,* 103–112.

Smith, Karen. (1998). Presentation at The Center for Inquiry, Columbia, SC.

Wells, G. (1986). *The meaning makers: Children learning language and using language to learn.* Portsmouth, NH: Heinemann.

Whitin, D. J., & Cox, R. (2003). *A mathematical passage: Strategies for promoting inquiry in grades 4–6.* Portsmouth, NH: Heinemann.

Whitin, D. J., Mills, H., & O'Keefe, T. (1990). *Living and learning mathematics: Stories and strategies for supporting mathematical literacy.* Portsmouth, NH: Heinemann.

Whitin, D. J., & Whitin, P. (2000). *Math is language too: Talking and writing in the mathematics classroom.* Urbana, IL/Reston, VA: National Council of Teachers of English and National Council of Teachers of Mathematics.

Wolk, S. (1998). *A democratic classroom.* Portsmouth, NH: Heinemann.

Yeager, B., Pattenaude, I., Fránquiz, M. E., & Jennings, L. B. (1999). Rights, respect, and responsibility: Toward a theory of action in two bilingual (Spanish/English) classrooms. In J. Robertson (Ed.), *Teaching for a Tolerant World, Grades K–6* (pp. 196–218). Urbana, IL: National Council of Teachers of English.

Children's Books Cited

Avi. (1995). *Poppy.* New York: Avon Books.

Birch, David. (1988). *The King's Chessboard.* New York: Dutton.

Bunting, E. (1988). *How many days to America? A Thanksgiving story.* New York: Clarion.

George, J. C. (1990). Birds' peace. In A. Durell & M. Sach (Eds), *The big book for peace.* New York: Dutton.

Hesse, K. (1996). *The music of dolphins.* New York: Scholastic.

Lewis, C. S. (1955). *The magician's nephew.* New York: Macmillan.

Lowry, L. (1990). The tree house. In A. Durell & M. Sachs (Eds.), *The big book for peace.* New York: Dutton.

Polacco, P. (1994). *Pink and Say.* New York: Philomel.

Polacco, P. (1998). *Thank you, Mr. Falker.* New York: Philomel.

Taylor, D. (Adapter). (2000). *A dream come true.* New York: Simon Spotlight/ Nickelodeon.

White, E. B. (1952). *Charlotte's web.* New York: Harper.

Yolen, Jane. (1977). *Owl moon.* New York: Scholastic.

Authors

Louise B. Jennings, Timothy O'Keefe, and Heidi Mills.   Photo by Alan Wieder.

Heidi Mills is professor of elementary education at the University of South Carolina. Her research interests include literacy, classroom inquiry, and teacher change. She is the curriculum and development specialist at the Center for Inquiry, a small school partnership, where she has been supporting and investigating the creation of inquiry-based curriculum within and across classrooms for the past seven years. Along with her Center for Inquiry colleagues, Mills has also been exploring the role of teacher study groups in developing a professional knowledge base. Additionally, she is a South Carolina Reading Initiative teaching team member. *Looking Closely and Listening Carefully* builds on Mills and O'Keefe's earlier collaborative research featured in *Looking Closely* (1992), a book focusing on the role of phonics in emergent literacy, coauthored with Diane Stephens. Mills has published four other books on literacy, mathematics, and inquiry-based instruction.

Timothy O'Keefe has been a classroom teacher for twenty-two years, from Head Start through sixth grade. As a teacher-researcher, he has written various chapters and articles in professional journals, and his classroom has been the focus of four books. O'Keefe's classroom has also been featured in a number of professional video series: Scienceline, a PBS series focusing on teaching science through inquiry; a series on teaching and reaching at-risk learners; a series focusing on literacy assessment strategies; and, most recently, a professional development series focusing on conversations in literature. O'Keefe has consulted with school districts throughout the country on topics such as inquiry-based instruction, developing integrated curricula, assessment strategies, and fostering parent communication. He is currently teaching at the Center for Inquiry, a small school partnership between Richland District Two and the University of South Carolina.

Louise B. Jennings is associate professor of social foundations of education and qualitative research methods at the University of South Carolina. A classroom and school ethnographer, her research explores how inquiry-based practices can contribute to a humanizing pedagogy and a critical democracy. Recent publications have appeared in the periodicals *Language Arts* and *Teachers College Record* and in the book *Teaching for a Tolerant World: Grades K–6* (1999). As a school ethnographer at the Center for Inquiry, Jennings closely followed one group of children from kindergarten through fifth grade. She also enjoys time with her husband, Gylton Da Matta, and their young son, Alex.

This book was typeset in Palatino and Helvetica by Electronic Imaging.
Typefaces used on the cover were Lucida Handwriting, Formata Medium,
and Garamond Light Condensed.
The book was printed on 60-lb. Accent Opaque Offset paper by Versa Press.